COOL CAREERS WITHOUT COLLEGE FOR

PEOPLE

WHO LOVE

HOUSES

COOL CAREERS WITHOUT COLLEGE FOR

PEOPLE

WHO LOVE

HOUSES

**ALICE
BECO**

The Rosen Publishing Group, Inc., New York

In memory of 32 Summerhill,
home of M, H, M, A, and J

Published in 2007 by The Rosen Publishing Group, Inc.
29 East 21st Street, New York, NY 10010

First Edition

Library of Congress Cataloging-in-Publication Data

Beco, Alice.
Cool careers without college for people who love houses/Alice Beco.
    p. cm.—(Cool careers without college)
Includes index.
ISBN 1-4042-0753-8 (library binding)
1. Home economics—Vocational guidance—Juvenile literature.
2. Dwellings—Maintenance and repair—Vocational guidance—Juvenile literature. I. Title. II. Series.

TX164.B43 2006
640.23—dc22
                                                            2005028666

Manufactured in the United States of America

CONTENTS

INTRODUCTION

"There's no place like home," declared Dorothy, the young ruby-slippered heroine of *The Wizard of Oz*. Few people would disagree. If we are lucky, our homes are shelters from the stress and chaos of the world outside. Home is where we relax and spend quality time with our family and friends. Homes are also extensions of who we are. Clean, well-built, nicely furnished, and beautifully decorated apartments and houses reflect the personalities of those who live there. They are unique environments in which we feel safe and comfortable and into which we welcome guests. Homes are also becoming secondary work spaces for an increasing number of people who work part-time or full-time out of their houses or apartments. This trend has created many new professional opportunities ranging from the design and decoration of home offices to the organization of filing and storage systems for home workers.

This book is for people who have a passion for homes—both their own and others'. People who perform the jobs described in this book spend their days in houses and apartments. They work closely with the objects, materials, and equipment that are used in the construction and maintenance of homes as well as with the people who own or rent them. In fact, one of the most rewarding aspects of many of these jobs is that they will permit you to come into contact with a wide range of interesting people. Furthermore, some of the jobs discussed can even be performed—at least in part—from your own home.

If you agree with the expression "Home is where the heart is," then you can imagine how essential the jobs listed here are to the homeowners and renters who will be your clients. Professionals who inspect, buy, sell, design, construct, repair, renovate, maintain, clean, organize, furnish, or decorate homes all perform services that have an important and positive impact on people's personal lives. Whether the home service you provide is temporary or ongoing, technical or creative, working with homes can be a satisfying and often profitable way to make a living. This book explores just a few of the various possibilities open to young people who are thinking of careers that don't require a college degree. Some occupations, such as painting and decorating, are popular ones that have existed for quite some time. Others, such as staging and organizing, are exciting new professions that have evolved as a result of our rapidly changing lifestyles.

HOUSEPAINTER

Many people like painting, but few consider turning it into a career. These days, being a housepainter involves more than showing up to work with a paintbrush, ladder, and bucket. Using an increasing array of sophisticated tools and techniques, housepainters apply paint, stain, varnish, and other finishes to homes in order to protect them

Painting a ceiling can be tricky. Even with the aid of scaffolding, it can be hard on a painter's back, neck, and arms. The golden rule in painting a ceiling is to never over stretch. To make the job easier, many painters use paint rollers that are equipped with a long extension handle.

and keep them looking attractive. Whether you spend your days outside or inside, painting homes can be an enjoyable way to make a living.

Description

Housepainters do more than simply splash paint on walls. They have to know what kind of supplies to select, depending on the surface to be covered. Surfaces can range from stucco walls and parquet floors to wooden fences and brick exteriors. After taking into consideration a home-owner's preferences, a painter decides what paints or finishes are most appropriate, attractive, and durable and how best to apply them.

Painters work for contractors, builders, or decorators, or are hired directly by homeowners. Sometimes, they might paint a house that has just been built. Other times, they will repaint a house that is being renovated or restored. Painters begin by measuring surfaces and calculating what materials (paint, chemicals, brushes, sponges, etc.) will be necessary. Based on their calculations of the estimated length of the project and the number of painters required, they present clients with a price.

Painters begin a job by preparing the surface that is going to be painted. Previous coats of paint or wallpaper need to be removed by stripping, sanding, wire brushing, burning, chemical cleaning, or water blasting. The techniques and equipment used will depend upon the particular surface. Blasting and chemical cleaning are usually for external brick and cement walls. Inside homes, it is necessary to wash all walls and moldings in order to remove dirt, dust, and grease. Cracks and holes should be patched and rough areas must be sanded down. Almost all painters will tell you that the secret to a good paint job is starting with a perfectly smooth surface.

A housepainter in Byron, Ohio, scrapes the old, peeling paint off a historic home. He will need to sand and smooth the exterior's surface before applying fresh paint and a finish that will protect the home from harsh weather and destructive pests such as pigeons and termites.

A painter chooses to apply paint not only based on the surface, but also the effect desired by the client. Some jobs might call for only a sponge or a good bristle brush with a soft edge. Other situations may require a pressure roller or a paint sprayer. Different tools create different textures. Special finishes or sealers provide protection from dirt and moisture.

Working with paint requires great precision and care as well as good hand-eye coordination. When working on a

Unusual Finishes

Paints are produced using sophisticated technology that was developed in the 1940s. However, when it comes to creating special effects, some professional painters discover that the simplest ingredients can yield surprising results. Sometimes, it's just a matter of opening your refrigerator. Mike Krawiec, who teaches painting techniques in the Chicago Area Painters and Decorators Joint Apprenticeship and Training Committee program, often finishes painted walls by using an inexpensive glaze he makes with a base of flat beer. Another trick is to make a marblelike glaze by mixing color pigment and 7-Up.

house with high ceilings or more than one floor, painters need to use a ladder or set up scaffolding—a metal pole structure that includes swing stages. A swing stage is a platform suspended by ropes or cables that are attached to a roof by large hooks.

As you can imagine, painters need agility and good balance. They also can't be afraid of heights. Being in good shape is essential since painters need to lift and move heavy furniture and scaffolding. They also spend a lot of time standing, bending, and reaching—repeated movements that put pressure on the back, legs, and arms. Painters use protective gear such as face masks, gloves, and coveralls to protect them from chemical substances and fumes.

Education and Training

Most housepainters get started by acquiring on-the-job experience. Painting rooms in your house or helping friends paint their family homes is an easy way to get started. Summer jobs with painting companies are excellent opportunities to learn the ropes by assisting experienced painters. Many small companies hire seasonal help. Other good places to gain experience are paint stores and interior decorating firms. In order to mix paints and match tones, it is important to have a good eye and a strong sense of color.

Although not necessary, you might consider an apprenticeship program that combines internships with classroom instruction. Common courses include use of tools and equipment, surface preparation, application techniques, paint mixing, wallpaper hanging, and blueprint reading. Apprenticeship programs usually last from two to four years. Candidates must be at least eighteen years old and have the equivalent of a high school diploma.

Experienced painters with strong business skills can become painting supervisors or even open up their own painting firms. Almost half of all painters are self-employed workers with their own businesses, while the other half are

It requires a great deal of care to paint decorative details such as medallions, moldings, and trim. Before applying paint, careful preparation is necessary. Surfaces need to be cleaned, and the area around the molding is frequently masked off with professional-quality tape. Smaller brushes, often with their bristles cut at an angle, are useful for getting paint into tight corners.

employed by painting firms or contracting companies involved in home construction, repair, and renovation.

Salary

Painters generally work forty-hour weeks and are paid by the hour, although overtime work during evenings and weekends may occur, thereby increasing earnings. In 2004, the average hourly wage for a housepainter was $16.

Outlook

While the rate of construction of new homes fluctuates depending on the real estate market and the economy, homeowners are increasingly engaged in the renovation and restoration of older houses. Nonetheless, many painters experience periods of unemployment, particularly during the winter, when painting exteriors can be difficult. Also, since most construction jobs last less than six weeks, there may be gaps between jobs when you earn no income. Life as a painter is rarely dull, however—you will be constantly traveling to different sites, meeting new clients, and undertaking new projects.

FOR MORE INFORMATION

ORGANIZATIONS

International Union of Painters and Allied Trades (IUPAT)
1750 New York Avenue NW
Washington, DC 20006
(202) 637-0700
Web site: http://www.iupat.org
   A labor organization for painters, paint makers, drywall finishers, paperhangers, decorators, and many other allied trades. In Canada and the United States, the union represents over 140,000 workers. Its Web site includes industry news, tips for workers, and job listings.

WEB SITES

Benjamin Moore Paints
http://www.benjaminmoore.com
> A colorful and fun site by a major North American paint company that has been in business since 1883. In addition to tips for homeowners and professionals, there are articles on the latest paints and equipment and a wealth of information about colors.

Old Masters
http://www.oldmastrs.com
> This maker of quality stains and finishes has created a Web site where you can download how-to guides for staining and finishing wood.

Sherwin-Williams
http://www.sherwin-williams.com
> Founded in 1866, Sherwin-Williams is North America's largest manufacturer of paints and finishes. This site features painting tips and information for homeowners and professionals,

BOOKS

Benjamin Moore & Company. *Exterior Style: Inspiring Color Ideas and Expert Painting Advice*. Boston, MA: Bulfinch Press, 2003.
> A thorough guide that explains how to prepare and paint exteriors of homes. Ideal for homeowners, painters, and decorators.

Dixon, Mark, and Bob Heidt. *House Painting: Inside and Out*. Newtown, CT: Taunton Press, 1997.
> A straightforward guide that tackles every aspect of the painting process.

Donegan, Francis. *Paint Your Home: Skills, Techniques, and Tricks of the Trade for Professional Looking Interior Painting*. Pleasantville, NY: Reader's Digest Association, 1997.
> A step-by-step guide to painting every room in a house with various tips from professionals.

Krim, Bonnie Rossier, and Judy Ostrow, eds. *Painting Your House Inside and Out: Tips and Techniques for Flawless Interiors and Exteriors.* San Diego, CA: Thunder Bay Press, 2003.
 A complete guide to color mixing and painting techniques for all kinds of surfaces. Includes many attractive photos.

McElroy, William. *Painter's Handbook.* Carlsbad, CA: Craftsman Book Company, 1987.
 Many professional painters swear by this book and consider it essential reading. It covers both the craft of painting and every aspect of how to start and run a professional business. Also included are specialty areas such as restoration and creating textured ceilings and murals.

Santos, Brian, and Ken Sidey, eds. *Painting Secrets.* Des Moines, IA: Meredith Books, 2004.
 This book focuses on the use of color and the painting process and explores various decorative techniques. It also includes a discussion of a wide range of tools and supplies.

PERIODICALS

PaintPRO
P.O. Box 25210
Eugene, OR 97402
(877) 935-8906 or (541) 341-3390
Web site: http://www.paintpro.net
 A bimonthly print and online trade magazine with tons of professional tips and advice on every aspect of painting.

2

HOUSE CLEANER

Are you a tidy person? Your cleanliness might not only please your parents but could lead to a promising career. Believe it or not, people are willing to pay a lot of money to have someone clean up their mess. If you are efficient, good at organizing, and not afraid of a physical workout, working as a house cleaner might be the career you're looking for. In

House cleaners should stay aware of cleaning equipment that can make their jobs quicker and easier. For instance, there are currently many types of specialty mops on the market that are designed to clean everything from venetian blinds to airplanes. The mop shown above is lighter than traditional cotton or sponge mops and doesn't leave lint on the floor.

general, you get to work in nice surroundings—the comfort of someone's home—in a situation that is nonstressful. With time, you might even build up your own cleaning business.

Description

To be a house cleaner, you need to have good cleaning skills. House cleaners are familiar with a large variety of cleaning products, know how to apply them, and are aware of the

Although in the past house cleaners were mostly women, in today's more diversified work environment, a growing number of men are offering their cleaning services. The cleaner shown above reveals a thoroughness and attention to detail that are essential. Not only does he vacuum the sofa's surface, he also cleans the dirt and dust beneath its cushions.

surfaces on which they can and can't be used. They must know how to operate equipment such as vacuum cleaners, washing machines, and irons.

House cleaners need to be physically fit since they spend a lot of time on their feet, reaching, bending, and lifting. The ability to take charge, work independently, and pay attention to detail is essential. Often, employees may be out all day.

Being trusted with their homes, fragile objects, prized possessions, and even pets is a big responsibility.

A good house cleaner is dependable, friendly, agreeable, discreet, and respectful of the privacy of his or her clients' homes. Some cleaners are lucky to work for people with whom they become quite friendly. If you work for clients who spend a lot of time at home, with time, close relationships can form and you'll find that you have become part of the family environment. This can make your job very agreeable.

Cleaning responsibilities depend on the agreement you work out with your employer—what he or she requires and what tasks you agree to perform. Basic cleaning may involve dusting, sweeping, mopping, vacuuming, washing, polishing (furniture, floors, and silverware), doing dishes and laundry, making beds, and tidying up. Sometimes you'll need to use chemical cleansers, bleaches, and other products. If not used carefully, these products can be dangerous to you and the environment, so knowledge of health and safety practices is necessary.

Some house cleaners iron clothes, sheets, and table linens and wash windows. In addition, they might even walk and feed pets, make meals and take care of children. Extra tasks usually lead to extra pay. Work schedules are often negotiated. While some people clean a different house every day, others prefer to work full-time throughout the week at one house (usually a large one).

Natural Solutions

Chemical cleansers can be harsh on surfaces and on your skin and respiratory system. Here are some green alternatives for common household problems:

- For a fresh-smelling refrigerator, place an open box of baking soda or a plate with sliced lemons on a back shelf.
- To leave a room smelling nice, pour some vanilla extract into a cup and let the scent diffuse throughout the room.
- To clean mirrors or glass, use a mixture of club soda and white vinegar as the cleaning agent and wipe with newspaper.
- To keep drains from clogging, pour boiling salted water down the pipes.
- To remove lipstick from fabrics, try rubbing toothpaste on the stains.
- To keep ants out, create a barrier by sprinkling cinnamon or black pepper in front of doorways.
- To polish copper, rub with ketchup and let it sit for five minutes before rinsing with hot water.

Source: Nontoxic Cleaning and Holistic Health Tips and Thensome Web page.
http://www.thensome.com/cleaning.htm

With consumers increasingly concerned about the toxic ingredients in many cleansers and detergents, a number of manufacturers are introducing "eco-friendly" products that use essential plant oils. Safe for the environment, they can also protect house cleaners from exposure to chemicals that can be harmful when touched or inhaled.

It is up to you to choose what kind of house (a mansion or an apartment) and what kind of client (a single working person or a big family) you would like to work for. Most house cleaners are self-employed; they work on their own and find their own clients. Some, however, work for commercial cleaning firms that send them out on assignments, sometimes in small teams. A few cleaners might actually live in the house where they work, receiving room and board as part of their payment.

Turnover among house cleaners tends to be high. Some cleaners work for short periods in order to earn extra money or to have a second income. Others move on to different types of work or start their own cleaning businesses.

Education and Training

No education or training is necessary to be a house cleaner. Most cleaners are simply naturally tidy people with some on-the-job experience. If you get a job cleaning part-time or during the summer for neighbors, this can provide you with experience and some useful letters of reference.

Salary

The average salary for a house cleaner in the United States is around $20,000 a year. Salaries can vary depending on skills, years of experience, and whether you supplement your cleaning with other tasks (such as cooking, ironing, and taking care of pets or children). Over time, you might want to open up your own cleaning business. If it grows successfully, you could end up managing a staff of cleaners and earning quite a good living.

Outlook

According to the U.S. Department of Labor, home cleaning is a rapidly growing field, particularly in big cities. As families with reasonable incomes become more pressed for time,

Some professional cleaners own businesses that specialize in specific jobs, such as cleaning windows or carpets. Carpet cleaners use various methods ranging from steaming and bonnet cleaning to shampooing and dry foam cleaning. All of these techniques involve applying some type of powder or solution to the carpet, allowing it to act, and then vacuuming the carpet until it is clean.

they are increasingly hiring house cleaners or cleaning services to perform a growing number of tasks in their houses and apartments. Furthermore, as the aging North American population continues to grow, older people will require cleaners to help them take care of their homes.

FOR MORE INFORMATION

ORGANIZATIONS

House Cleaning Association
865 North Decatur Street
Denver, CO 80204
(877) 865-6700 or (303) 974-2810
Web site: http://www.house-cleaning-association.com
> This association of independent housecleaning companies located throughout the United States offers help in training and marketing. It also provides access to online news and discussion groups.

WEB SITES

AllAboutHome.com by ServiceMaster
http://www.allabouthome.com/directories/dir_cleaning.html
> Cleaning "artists" offer tips for everything from cleaning up after pets to removing stains and scum from bathroom tiles. Also includes a list of professional cleaners.

Cleaning.com
http://www.cleaning.com
> This site provides a wide range of cleaning resources and information ranging from a professional cleaner database and an online product store to cleaning tips, lessons, and news and articles for professionals.

Food Fun and Facts: Household Hints and Cleaning Tips
http://www.foodfunandfacts.com/householdhints.htm
> A site that offers instructions on everything from bed making and book care to tips on polishing various surfaces and doing laundry.

The Frugal Housekeeper
http://www.nd.edu/~abigger
> Articles for amateur and professional cleaners with lots of cost-cutting cleaning tips and techniques.

Mary Moppins Cleaning System
http://www.goclean.com
> Mary Findley invented her own mop and cleaning system designed to help cleaners save time and reduce waste. Her Web site includes cleaning tips for every room in a home, as well as a stain removal guide.

Nontoxic Cleaning and Holistic Health Tips and Thensome
http://www.thensome.com/cleaning.htm
> This down-to-earth site with an emphasis on stains and problems created by pets, specializes in environmentally friendly, basic, and sometimes surprising household cleaning tips.

Queen of Clean
http://www.queenofclean.com/tips
> Have a tough cleaning problem? Linda Cobb, "The Queen of Clean," can help with her many tips, tricks, and hints.

Removing Stains at Home
http://www.human.cornell.edu/txa/outreach/upload/removingstains.pdf
> Cornell University's Department of Textiles and Apparel offers a fifteen-page pamphlet with precise directions for removing every kind of stain imaginable from numerous fabrics and surfaces. All solutions are pretested in Cornell's laboratories in Ithaca, NY.

BOOKS
Aslett, Don. *The Cleaning Encyclopedia*. New York, NY: Dell, 1999.
> Guidance on how to clean almost everything imaginable without causing damage.

Bewsey, Susan. *Start and Run a Home Cleaning Business*. 2nd ed. Vancouver, BC: Self-Counsel Press, 2003.
> This book gives advice on how to start a cleaning business and survive the crucial first year. The accompanying CD-ROM comes with numerous forms to get you started.

Bredenberg, Jeff. *Clean It Fast, Clean It Right: The Ultimate Guide to Making Absolutely Everything You Own Sparkle and Shine*. Emmaus, PA: Rodale Books, 1999.
> More than 250 experts explain how to clean over 300 common household items, ranging from floors (with advice from the cleanup crew for the Los Angeles Lakers basketball team) to paintings (with tips from a conservator at New York's Guggenheim Museum).

Haley, Graham, and Rosemary Haley. *Haley's Cleaning Hints*. New York, NY: New American Library, 2004.
> A practical and good-humored guide that offers more than 1,000 ways to clean and organize a home using regular household products that have multiple cleaning and stain-removing abilities.

Morse, Melinda, and Laura Jorstad. *How to Start a Home-Based Housecleaning Business*. Guilford, CT: Globe Pequot, 2002.
> This book discusses money-saving strategies for launching and building your own home-based cleaning business. It combines expert advice with personal experiences: author Morse started her own successful cleaning business to help pay for graduate school.

Ward, Schar. *Coming Clean: Dirty Little Secrets from a Professional Housecleaner*. Minnetonka, MN: Book Peddlers, 2002.
> Simple and practical strategies for maintaining a clean and well-organized home.

3

BED-AND-BREAKFAST OPERATOR

As the operator of a bed-and-breakfast, you can work at home and live in the house of your dreams. "B&B" operators work at creating an original and welcoming atmosphere that allows their guests to feel completely at home. If you like being a host and meeting new people from all around the world, running a B&B could be the perfect job for you.

Innkeeper Dina Brigish stands outside her bed-and-breakfast, the White Pig, located in a historic farmhouse in Schulyer, Virginia. Brigish attended a natural cooking school in New York and turned her inn into a "vegetarian retreat," offering guests gourmet vegan and vegetarian meals, such as egg-free omelets and soy bacon. The inn has received an award from the People for the Ethical Treatment of Animals (PETA) for promoting animal-friendly service.

Description

A bed-and-breakfast is basically a person's home that operates as a small guesthouse or inn. Visitors often prefer B&Bs to hotels because they are cozier and offer a friendly, home-away-from-home atmosphere. Usually less expensive than big hotels, B&Bs allow guests to come into contact with people from different places.

An appealing aspect about running a B&B is that you—and your friends, family, or partners, if you choose to have associates—get to be your own boss. If you prefer to work autonomously as opposed to working for others, you will enjoy your independence as a bed-and-breakfast operator. Another benefit is that since you are running a business in your home, many costs—such as electricity, water, heating, telephone, cable television, decoration, and repairs—count as work expenses and can be deducted as such on your taxes. Depending on how many rooms you choose to rent out, running a B&B can supply you with part-time or full-time income. If your business is seasonal—if you own a beach house that draws in vacationers in the spring, summer, and fall, for instance—you can close down and enjoy your free time during the off-season.

To run a successful bed-and-breakfast, you have to be able to communicate well with people and also be fairly knowledgeable about houses. Although you can hire professionals such as plumbers and electricians to fix things that go wrong, it helps if you have some background in household maintenance. Since B&Bs provide breakfast for their guests, it is also useful to be a good cook. You have to be attentive to all your guests' needs and maintain a welcoming atmosphere in which everything is clean and functions perfectly. An eye for detail is essential. Diplomacy, patience, and understanding are required—not all guests will be pleasant or easy to please.

Inn-sitting

What do you do if you're a B&B owner and you want to go on vacation? Get an inn sitter, of course. Inn sitters are substitute innkeepers who take over an inn for a temporary period and make sure everything runs smoothly in the owner's absence. For aspiring B&B owners, this can be an ideal educational experience. At the same time, you can earn an income and take advantage of an opportunity to travel.

Although this can mean being on call twenty-four hours a day, much of your work will consist of enjoyable tasks such as preparing meals (most B&Bs include only breakfast), chatting with guests, and helping plan their outings and itineraries. However, keep in mind that a B&B is a business. After acquiring a license, permit, and insurance, you will need to figure out how to make money. There are many things to consider: how many guests you will be able to

A special breakfast is only one of the personalized services guests receive when staying at the East Brother Light Station, a bed-and-breakfast located in a 130-year-old, fully functioning lighthouse on California's East Brother Island. A unique combination of both a "lighthouse B&B" and an "island B&B," the inn feels as if it's a world away, but it is only a ten-minute boat ride from San Francisco.

lodge, the price of room and board, any extra services offered (ranging from translation and guided tours to baby-sitting and pet care), what size staff you might need, and what your reservation policy will be. You'll also need to think about marketing your B&B. This includes advertising at local tourist bureaus, in travel magazines, and through reservation agencies or B&B brokers (companies that will promote your B&B and take reservations for you). By creating your own Web site, you can advertise and take reservations on the Internet.

Education and Training

Starting a B&B requires very little capital (money) or experience and no formal education or training. You might begin by redecorating an extra room in your home. Although rules may vary by state, as long as you're hosting overnight visitors on a small scale (one or two guests at a time), you usually don't even need a license. (You do need a license to serve food, however.)

Most bed-and-breakfast operators gain their experience on the job. To set your B&B apart from the competition, you should have original services and decor. Courses in hotel management or tourism from a technical school or community college can be useful, but they aren't necessary. Skills learned from cooking classes will allow you to impress guests with your culinary abilities, and language courses could come in handy if you expect to receive foreign visitors. Keeping up to date with travel literature, such as guide

Furnishings and decorative details give a B&B a distinctive character. The Sweetwater Farm Bed and Breakfast in Glen Mills, Pennsylvania, features twelve guest rooms located in an eighteenth-century farmhouse and adjoining wing. While antiques reflect the inn's history, personalized touches, such as extra pillows, attractive lighting, and books and magazines, help make guests feel pampered and at home.

books, travel magazines, and related Web sites, to see what makes other inns and B&Bs successful is very useful (visiting them is even better). It is also important to stay attuned to what is happening in the global travel industry. Part-time or summer jobs in the service or travel industry—working in cafés, restaurants, hotels, or on cruise ships—can give you valuable experience. Another great way to learn the ropes is by working as an inn sitter.

Travel Facts

- In 2003, 13.9 million overseas travelers stayed in American hotels, motels, or B&Bs for an average of 7.5 nights.

- Of vacationers staying in hotels, 47 percent check in for one night, 26 percent stay for two nights, and 27 percent spend three or more nights.

- Forty-five percent of all vacationing hotel guests are between thirty-five and fifty-four years old.

- One out of every eight Americans is employed directly or indirectly in the travel industry.

- In 2003, domestic and international travelers in the United States spent a total average of $1.5 billion a day.

(Note: All statistics are based on 2003 figures.)

Source: U.S. Department of Commerce, International Trade Administration, Office of Travel and Tourism Industries; D.K. Shifflet & Associates, Ltd; Travel Industry Association of America.

Salary

Your income as a bed-and-breakfast operator will depend upon the size of your B&B, the number of rooms you rent, how many vacancies you have, and the prices you charge for the space and services you provide. The more efficient you are at running your B&B—cutting costs while maximizing income—the more money you are likely to make.

Outlook

The United States receives more revenue from international tourists than any other country in the world. As people travel more and continue to seek increasingly specialized lodgings and services, the hospitality industry will continue to experience new opportunities for growth. B&Bs are well suited to the rising number of budget travelers who have less time to travel but seek a personalized, unique, and homey atmosphere instead of the anonymity of a large hotel chain.

B&B operators must be able to adapt to external circumstances. For example, in difficult economic times, people have less money to spend on vacations and business trips. Natural and man-made disasters in a specific region can also affect the hotel business. Hurricanes, earthquakes, and other catastrophes can result in cancelled reservations. Criminal activity and fear of violence can also cause travelers to change their plans.

FOR MORE INFORMATION

ORGANIZATIONS

Educational Institute of the American Hotel and Lodging Association
800 N. Magnolia Avenue, Suite 1800
Orlando, FL 32853-1126
(800) 752-4567 or (407) 999-8100
Web site: http://www.ei-ahla.org
> Offers a large array of educational videos, DVDs, books, guides, seminars, and training programs that focus on aspects ranging from exceptional guest service to bookkeeping.

WEB SITES

American Bed and Breakfast Association (ABBA)
http://www.abba.com
> This association is dedicated to promoting bed-and-breakfasts by offering listings of B&Bs throughout the United States, organized by locality and region.

Bed and Breakfast Online Canada
http://www.bbcanada.com
> Includes all sorts of information ranging from a list of properties for sale and useful books and magazines to links and tips for starting and managing your own B&B. It also features a list of Canadian B&Bs, organized according to geographic region.

Hospitality Jobs Online
http://www.hospitalityonline.com
> This job site for the hospitality industry features career news, listings, and tips on preparing for an interview and writing a résumé.

I Love Inns
http://www.iloveinns.com
> American Historic Inns publishes B&B guidebooks and runs iloveinns.com. The site features articles and reviews of B&Bs, as well as a directory of thousands of B&Bs—from historic to modern—located across the United States It also includes listings of B&Bs that are for sale.

The Rooms Chronicle
http://www.roomschronicle.com
> This site is dedicated to hotel management. Interesting articles discuss everything from people skills and handling complaints to lowering energy costs and housekeeping.

BOOKS

Arduser, Lora, and Douglas R. Brown. *How to Open a Financially Successful Bed and Breakfast or Small Hotel*. Ocala, FL: Atlantic Publishing, 2004.
> This handbook tells you everything you need to know about running a successful B&B or inn. An accompanying CD-ROM provides samples of useful business plans.

Cozzens, Michele Vanort. *I'm Living Your Dream Life: The Story of a Northwoods Resort Owner*. Indian Wells, CA: McKenna Publishing Group, 2002.
> A humorous memoir and how-to guide about a family that left the big city to open a B&B in the woods of northern Wisconsin.

Craig, Susannah, and Park Davis. *The Complete Idiot's Guide to Running a Bed and Breakfast*. Indianapolis, IN: Alpha Books, 2001.
> This thorough sourcebook about opening and running a successful B&B includes how to choose a profitable location, how to create business plans and Web sites, and what services to offer. It also helps you judge whether running a B&B is really the right career choice for you.

Hardy, Pat, Jo Ann M. Bell, Mary E. Davies, and Susan Brown, eds. *So You Want to Be an Innkeeper: The Definitive Guide to Operating a Successful Bed-and-Breakfast or Country Inn.* 4th ed. San Francisco, CA: Chronicle Books, 2004.

> This best-selling book by four B&B owners offers good information on the business aspects involved in running a B&B. The personality traits needed to be a successful innkeeper are also discussed.

Stankus, Jan. *How to Open and Operate a Bed and Breakfast.* 4th ed. Guilford, CT: Globe Pequot Press, 2000.

> A comprehensive handbook that focuses on how to start a B&B and how to juggle being an innkeeper with your personal life.

PERIODICALS

Arrington's Bed & Breakfast Journal

214 W. Texas, Suite 400
Midland, TX 79701
Web site: http://www.bnbjournal.com

> A leading monthly trade magazine for innkeepers, inn sitters, and those wanting to own their own B&Bs. Includes expert advice, trends, and reviews. The online version features articles, recipes, a calendar of hotel industry conferences, and lists of B&Bs for sale.

North American Inns: Bed & Breakfast and Resorts

Harworth Publishing
P.O. Box 998
Guelph, ON N1H 6N1
Canada
Web site: http://www.bbcanada.com/bb_marketplace/magazines/nai

> This magazine, published four times a year, offers articles, ideas, and recipes for innkeepers as well as articles with a special focus on Canadian inns and B&Bs.

4

HOME DECORATOR

Most teenagers want to personalize their rooms. They often do so by putting up art and arranging things in their own manner. Some, however, also want to pick out paint colors, bed linens, and furniture. A few even start giving advice to their parents about the rest of the house. Sound familiar? Are you someone that has always enjoyed decorating or redecorating your room

and (if your parents let you) other rooms in the house? Do you like meeting new people and using your creativity? If so, you might want to consider a career as a home decorator.

Description

Home decorators furnish and accessorize the interiors of people's houses and apartments according to the vision their clients have of the ideal home. Using their own experience, knowledge, and creative flair, decorators help decide what color a room's walls should be painted, what fabrics should be used for a sofa or chair, and what pieces of furniture might look good together and how they should be arranged. Some decorators tackle entire houses or apartments, while others specialize in specific rooms, such as bathrooms, kitchens, or children's rooms.

As a decorator, you will begin by consulting with your clients. You'll analyze their needs and their budget. Based on this information, you'll develop a proposal. Since you're working with your clients' homes, your main goal is to win their approval of your decorating plans. Proposals take into consideration space planning or layout, furniture, lighting,

The paint colors inside a home can set mood, accent features, hide faults, and reflect the homeowner's personality. However, choosing color combinations can be a difficult task. A color wheel is an important tool of the decorating trade and can help show how colors relate to one another and whether they clash or harmonize.

color schemes, wall coverings and wallpaper, paint, fabrics, flooring, door and window treatments, and use of accessories such as pillows, carpets, plants, and art works. Many decorators work directly with new homeowners or with people who want to redecorate an older dwelling. Others, however, work with decorating or design firms or with homebuilders.

Professional decorators should develop good relationships with suppliers of the products and services they need. These include manufacturers of furniture, flooring, lighting fixtures, and fabrics, as well as painters, carpenters, and electricians. Decorators are not only responsible for purchasing furnishings and accessories, but also for overseeing the jobs performed by other specialized workers and tradespeople.

Education and Training

No professional training is required to become a home decorator. However, it is helpful to have some background in art and math (exact measurements and precise calculations are necessary). Since most home decorators are self-employed, some business skills are useful, as are effective communication skills for dealing with clients. The ability to multitask is beneficial since decorators often work on more than one project at a time. Most important of all, however, is a good eye for design and a strong sense of color.

Some decorators are also designers or artists who contribute their particular artistic talents to their clients. For instance, as part of the decorating plan for a family's living room, decorator Sam Harris of Waynesboro, Virginia, designed and painted a ceiling mural.

Most decorators train themselves by taking decorating courses at art schools or community colleges, consulting Web sites, reading home decorating and architectural magazines, and speaking to furnishings retailers. This will help you to familiarize yourself with different styles and stay up to date with new trends. Visiting design museums and home shows is also useful. In addition, it is a good idea to build up your own library of decorating books and magazines that you can use for reference. Ask your parents or

Siblings with Style

David Adler (1882–1949) and Frances Adler (1888–1953) grew up in Milwaukee, Wisconsin, at the end of the nineteenth century. After finishing high school and college, David studied architecture in Europe and then began designing traditional country homes for wealthy American clients. After high school, Frances

Decorator Frances Elkins often worked on projects with her architect brother. While he was a traditionalist, she broke many decorating "rules." For example, she mixed classical antiques with unusual contemporary furniture that was designed by avant-garde artists and made from non-traditional materials.

married a polo player named Felton Elkins and moved to California. When she divorced her husband in 1918, Frances had no means of supporting herself and her young daughter. A stylish and creative woman, her solution was to begin decorating houses for friends. Before long, she was decorating the homes of big Hollywood personalities, such as Edward G. Robinson (a classic film actor known for his gangster roles) and David O'Selznick (the producer of *Gone with the Wind*).

Her more reserved brother didn't approve of her flashy clients and extravagant decorative touches. He also thought Frances bossed around her clients too much—telling them how to set their tables and what kind and color of flowers to buy (pink and red carnations). Nevertheless, David did admire her taste. Together, brother and sister collaborated on many homes and traveled to Europe to buy furniture. Sadly, only one of their joint projects remains intact today: a house in Lake Forest, Illinois, where Frances lined the library walls entirely in goatskin!

(Source: Eve M. Kahn. "A 28-Year Love Affair with a Pair of Stylish Siblings," New York Times, June 2, 2005. Retrieved online at: http://www.nytimes.com/2005/06/02/garden/02elkins.html?ex=1275364800&en=75e4267cbd3b7c39&ei=5088&partner=rssnyt&emc=rss).

friends if you can decorate a room for free. Take before and after photographs of your work so that you begin creating a portfolio to show future clients.

You can also gain experience and meet potential clients by getting a part-time or full-time job in the industry. Companies that hire interns who are exposed to some aspect of decoration include furniture and housewares manufacturers, retailers (stores selling furniture, antiques, design objects, or home furnishings), and decorating firms.

Salary

Home decorators can make anywhere between $20,000 and $40,000 a year. A top-notch decorator with a good reputation, formal training, and a list of wealthy clients can make $70,000 a year, or even more. Some of these decorators work for interior design firms or furniture retailers that pay them high salaries. Others have their own small decorating businesses. However, most decorators are freelancers who often work from their own homes. Clients' smaller budgets as well as possible gaps between projects mean that freelancers tend to have lower incomes.

Outlook

At present, the rising demand for professionally designed homes is creating more need for home decorators. The U.S.

North America's most famous decorator, Martha Stewart, has always believed that style should be available at discount prices. In 1997, she launched a brand of affordable home decorating products, called Martha Stewart Everyday, at Kmart stores. The products range from lamps and mirrors to a line of subtle paint shades, called "colors," shown here.

Department of Labor predicts that jobs for home decorators could increase by as much as 22 percent in the next few years. However, as more people are attracted to design-related careers, there will also be more competition for these jobs. The more training and experience you have, the better your chances of success in the field.

FOR MORE INFORMATION

ORGANIZATIONS

Canadian Decorators' Association (CDECA)
P.O. Box 31037
475 Westney Road North
Ajax, ON L1T 3V2
Canada
(888) 233-2248
Web site: http://www.cdeca.com
   Includes information and resources for Canada's association of professional decorators and designers.

Certified Interior Decorators International (CID)
649 SE Central Parkway
Stuart, FL 34994
(772) 287-1855
Web site: http://www.cidinternational.org
   This association offers education and certification programs for professional decorators.

WEB SITES

Canadian Interior Design
http://www.canadianinteriordesign.com
   This fun site has thousands of photos of decorating and design solutions with an emphasis on new ideas and trends.

HGTV (Home & Garden Television) Online
http://www.hgtv.com/hgtv/decorating/0,1792,HGTV_3545,00.html
   This Web site of one of North America's most popular cable networks has a great selection of information, links, discussion forums, and photos related to decorating or remodeling any room in your house.

Home and Family Network
http://www.homeandfamilynetwork.com/decorating/index.html
Consists of hundreds of decorating ideas and projects, design lessons, and photos of home makeovers.

BOOKS

Bradbury, Dominic. *American Designers' Houses*. New York, NY: Vendome Press, 2004.
A coffee-table book that takes readers on tours of the homes of twenty of today's leading interior designers. The text includes interviews with the designers.

Campbell, Nina. *Nina Campbell's Decorating Notebook: Insider Secrets and Decorating Ideas for Your Home*. New York, NY: Clarkson Potter, 2004.
This title offers a glimpse into the job requirements of a professional decorator. Campbell shares personal stories as she seeks creative solutions to practical problems. The text is accompanied by many before and after photos.

Coleman, Brian D. *Extraordinary Interiors: Decorating with Architectural Salvage and Antiques.* Layton, UT: Gibbs Smith Publishers, 2005.
An offering of original ideas on how to decorate inexpensively by reusing and preserving furniture and other salvaged pieces from old buildings, businesses, and homes.

Goulet, Tag, and Catherine Goulet. *FabJob Guide to Becoming an Interior Decorator.* Seattle, WA: Fabjob.com, 2003.
Available in print or on CD-ROM, this step-by-step introductory guide explains how to get started in the decorating business. It briefly covers a wide variety of decorating topics.

Salny, Stephen M. *Frances Elkins: Interior Design*. New York, NY: Norton, 2005.
A biography of Frances Adler Elkins, an avant-garde decorator who, along with her famous architect brother, David Adler, worked with numerous Hollywood stars.

PERIODICALS

Canadian Interiors
Crailer Communications
360 Dupont Street
Toronto, ON M5R 1V9
Canada
Web site: http://www.canadianinteriors.com/current.htm
   Print and online interior design magazine with original and
   informative features that boast a strong Canadian content.

Domino
Condé Nast Publications
4 Times Square, 17th Floor
New York, NY 10036
Web site: http://www.dominomag.com
   A magazine that is like a personal shopper for those seeking to
   redecorate or renovate their homes. It features decorative objects
   and furnishings for every style and price range and indicates where
   to get them.

Elle Decor
Hachette Filipacchi Media
1633 Broadway
New York, NY 10019
Web site: http://www.elledecor.com
   This stylish print magazine with beautiful photos includes articles
   and tips on the latest trends in home design and living.

Home Magazine
Hachette Filipacchi Media
1633 Broadway
New York, NY 10019
Web site: http://www.homemag.com
   A magazine that offers practical and affordable decorating solutions
   and examples of home makeovers, including before and after photos.

House & Garden
Condé Nast Publications
4 Times Square, 17th Floor
New York, NY 10036
Web site: http://www.houseandgarden.com
   This upmarket glossy magazine features attractive photos and
   numerous resources for decorating and landscaping.

Martha Stewart Living
11 West 42nd Street, 25th Floor
New York, NY 10036
Web site: http://www.marthastewart.com
   A print and online magazine that focuses on different aspects of
   home decoration and entertaining.

Metropolitan Home
Hachette Filipacchi Media
1633 Broadway
New York, NY 10019
Web site: http://www.neodata.com/hfmus/mhme
   Print and online versions of this magazine feature decorating
   tips and secrets from the world's most renowned designers and
   decorators.

5

INTERIOR DESIGNER

When you walk into a store, a restaurant, or a friend's house, do you pay close attention to space, lighting, colors, and furnishings, and how they work together to create a beautiful and functional environment? Do you imagine how you could make these spaces more visually appealing? If such a challenge sounds tempting, you might want to consider becoming an interior designer.

Pier Luigi Pizzi is an Italian director as well as a stage and costume designer who has worked on important theatrical productions around the world. Stage set design obviously influenced him when he set about designing and decorating his own home *(above)* in Venice, Italy. The monumental pillars and sculptures in the vast living room, with their bold shapes and contrasting shades of light and dark, create a distinctly theatrical setting.

Description

Interior designers work with other professionals and home-owners to create design solutions for homes that meet the needs and reflect the lifestyles of their clients. Aside from being creative and artistic, designers must have business skills and be good at communicating and working with others. Some designers are self-employed, but many work for design firms with several employees. Large interior design firms employ anywhere from 50 to 100 designers. Some designers also get jobs with furniture and home-furnishing stores and architecture firms.

Aside from having a background in art and design, interior designers must know how to plan a space and how to present this plan to their clients—both visually (via sketches or computer graphics) and in words. Whereas decorators are involved with decorating a home's interior, designers deal with the overall design and construction of a house. As an interior designer, you'll need to understand how different materials and products are used and how elements such as color, light, scale, and texture work together to create a specific environment. Designers must know about acoustics (the transmission and echo of sound) as well as ergonomics, which is the science of using information about human beings to design spaces fit for their needs. A solid understanding of technical concerns such as the stability of a house's structure, safety procedures, fire-safety requirements, and building codes (national, state, and local) is also essential. You must be able to make decisions such as where to knock down a wall and what kind of staircase to build.

As a designer, you must be comfortable dealing with people's very different needs and personalities. You must not only be a good communicator but also a good listener, since you need to be able to understand exactly what your

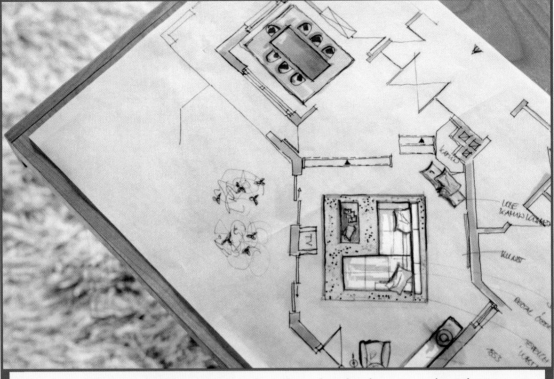

The first thing a designer must do when beginning a project is to consider the affected space. Drawing a floor plan with accurate dimensions provides a bird's-eye view of an entire room, house, or apartment. After examining the space and its possible limitations, furniture can be added and arranged on paper to see what will create a harmonious environment.

client wants (sometimes he or she might have difficulty expressing his or her desires). Being able to work with others is important, since designers often collaborate with architects, builders, engineers, electricians, plumbers, and many other specialists. You must be open to changes demanded by your clients and good at solving problems.

Good management skills are essential since most designers work on tight deadlines and often juggle more

Q & A with a Working Pro

Tina Glavan is an interior designer for the architect William T. Georgis in New York City.

Q: IS SOMEONE BORN WITH A DESIGNER'S EYE OR CAN IT BE DEVELOPED?
A: *I feel you're kind of born with it. You can be taught the technicalities, but it's what you do with them that make you a designer.*

Q: HOW DID YOU GET STARTED?
A: *By chance. I took an interior design class with a friend and liked it, so I decided to continue and get a second degree. When I graduated, I got a job through the school's job office and landed in a prestigious architectural firm.*

Q: WHAT ARE THE BEST AND WORST PARTS ABOUT YOUR JOB?
A: *The worst are deadlines, long hours, scheduling, delays. The best? Seeing it all come together at the end and seeing the client's face for the first time when they walk into their new home.*

Q: WHAT IS THE MOST IMPORTANT QUALITY FOR A SUCCESSFUL DESIGNER?

A: Knowing how to listen to your clients' needs and wants and being capable of interpreting them into the design of a room or home.

Q: DID YOU EVER MAKE A REALLY BIG DESIGN MISTAKE? HOW DID YOU FIX IT?

A: Yes. You don't do it again! Basically, you learn from your mistakes and do it over.

Interior designer Tina Glavan believes that a good designer's most important quality is the ability to really listen to a client's needs and then to successfully interpret them into the design of a home.

than one project at a time. Knowing how to market yourself and your strengths is important, since a key part of your job will be presenting and selling your ideas to new clients in ways that are informative and imaginative.

Education and Training

In some states and provinces, you cannot call yourself an interior designer unless you have taken the following three steps. The first involves acquiring some specialized education by taking courses from an institution such as an art or design school. The institution's interior design program must be recognized by the Foundation for Interior Design Education Research (FIDER). Subjects studied usually include interior design, art, architecture, lighting, materials and textiles, business, and marketing. The second step is on-the-job experience with a certified designer or architect, which will help you build up a portfolio of work. Many young designers start out as assistants to designers or architects—they do project research and draw up design plans. The final step is to pass a certifying exam given by the National Council for Interior Design Qualification (NCIDQ). This is valid in both Canada and the United States. Presently, in eighteen American states, it is against the law to call yourself an interior designer if you are not certified. After passing this exam, you must follow all the professional standards required by the American

Society of Interior Designers (ASID) or the Interior Designers of Canada (IDC).

Salary

A designer's earnings depend on many factors. These include number of years of experience and reputation. Another factor is whether a designer freelances or earns a regular salary at a large design firm with a permanent client list. According to the U.S. Bureau of Labor Statistics, on average, designers who are just starting out (whether at a firm or as freelancers) earn between $20,000 and $25,000 a year. Designers who have some experience and are also good at managing projects and communicating with clients can make between $50,000 and $70,000 a year.

Outlook

The demand for designers tends to vary depending on the state of the economy. In the near future, the U.S. Bureau of Labor Statistics predicts jobs for designers will grow significantly. However, competition for the best-paying jobs will be high. Designers with the most education and strongest business skills as well as talent and determination have the best chance of succeeding.

FOR MORE INFORMATION

ORGANIZATIONS

American Society of Interior Designers (ASID)
National Headquarters
608 Massachusetts Avenue NE
Washington, DC 20002
(202) 546-3480
Web site: http://www.asid.org
> This community of designers, industry representatives, educators, and design students promotes education, events, discussions, and debates related to design.

Foundation for Interior Design Education Research (FIDER)
146 Monroe Center NW, Suite 1318
Grand Rapids, MI 49503-2822
(616) 458-0400
Web site: http://www.fider.org
> FIDER is a nonprofit organization that sets standards for interior design courses and certifies academic programs that meet those standards throughout Canada and the United States.

Interior Design Educators Council (IDEC)
7150 Winton Drive, Suite 300
Indianapolis, IN 46268
(317) 328-4437
Web site: http://www.idec.org
> IDEC promotes information and research exchange about all areas of interior design.

Interior Designers of Canada (IDC)
717 Church Street
Toronto, ON M4W 2M5

Canada
(416) 594-9310
Web site: http://www.interiordesigncanada.org
> Canada's national association of designers works with its provincial associations to create standards and educational programs. It also fosters an exchange of information and ideas for anyone interested in design.

National Council for Interior Design Qualification (NCIDQ)
1200 18th Street NW, Suite 1001
Washington, DC 20036-2506
(202) 721-0220
Web site: http://www.ncidq.org
> This nonprofit organization sets professional standards for interior designers in Canada and the United States.

WEB SITES

Careers in Interior Design
http://www.careersininteriordesign.com/index.html
> Includes information and resources for those interested in an interior design career.

BOOKS

Gilliatt, Mary. *Mary Gilliatt's Interior Design Course* (Décor Best-Sellers). New York, NY: Watson-Guptill Publications, 2001.
> A step-by-step guide to understanding the basic elements of good design and solving specific design problems. Useful for both beginners and professionals.

Lynch, Sarah. *77 Habits of Highly Creative Interior Designers: Insider Secrets from the World's Top Design Professionals* (Interior Design and Architecture). Gloucester, MA: Rockport Publishers, 2003.
> Lynch's straightforward and useful guide features a panel of professional designers and architects who give expert advice on a variety of topics related to design.

Pile, John F. *Interior Design.* 3rd ed. Englewood Cliffs, NJ: Prentice
    Hall, 2003.
    For designers who are just starting out in the field, this is an
    updated version of one of the leading textbooks used by interior
    design students at art school.
Piotrowski, Christine. *Becoming an Interior Designer.* Hoboken, NJ:
    John Wiley and Sons, 2004.
    A practical guide written for people interested in or starting out in
    a design career. Emphasis is placed on training, education, and
    how to get hired.
Susanka, Sarah. *Home by Design.* Newtown, CT: Taunton Press, 2004.
    Susanka, a renowned architect, explores various solutions that are
    used in well-designed homes.

PERIODICALS

Canadian Interiors
Crailer Communications
360 Dupont Street
Toronto, ON M5R 1V9
Canada
Web site: http://www.canadianinteriors.com/current.htm
    A print and online magazine devoted to interior design. Its articles
    have an emphasis on Canadian homes and buildings.

Dwell
99 Osgood Place
San Francisco, CA 94133
Web site: http://www.dwellmag.com
    Print and online versions of this cutting-edge magazine explore
    new trends and concepts in international architecture and design.

Fine Homebuilding
Taunton Press
63 South Main Street

P.O. Box 5506
Newtown, CT 06470-5506
Web site: http://www.taunton.com/finehomebuilding/index.asp
This practical magazine offers how-to advice for every aspect of building, repairing, and renovating a home—from decorating tips to information on power tools. An online version contains archives and discussion groups.

Inspired House
Taunton Press
63 South Main Street
P.O. Box 5506
Newtown, CT 06470-5506
Web site: http://www.taunton.com/inspiredhouse/index.asp
A bimonthly magazine that is filled with practical solutions and lots of in-depth information on renovating or remodeling a house. It includes discussions of different building and decorating materials.

Interior Design
Reed Business Information Multimedia
360 Park Avenue South
New York, NY 10010
Web site: http://www.interiordesign.net
This magazine features new trends, ideas, products, and industry information for professional designers. Includes lots of interviews and attractive photos.

HOME
INSPECTOR

Do you like detective work? Being a home inspector is kind of like being a detective. Using acquired knowledge about building structures, you get to examine other people's homes for an important reason: to make sure they are safe and in good condition. By examining every part of a home, an inspector can discover flaws and potential problems and warn interested buyers. This can lead to a significant reduction in the price of an apartment or house. It can also ensure that dreams of home ownership don't turn into nightmares.

Description

Home inspection is a fairly new profession. Originally, many people shopping for a home relied on builder and architect friends to provide them with knowledgeable opinions about the condition of a house. However, in the 1970s, buyers increasingly began turning to specialists who were trained to look at much more than major structural problems, such as leaking pipes and sinking foundations. These experts became known as home inspectors. They are hired to comb houses from top to bottom, checking everything from plumbing, electrical wiring, roofing, and ventilation to major kitchen appliances and heating and cooling systems.

As an inspector, you must be able to identify current flaws as well as predict future concerns. Your subsequent report will include the estimated cost of fixing these problems so that the buyer will know how much he or she will need to invest in repairs. Sometimes the seller of a house will hire a home inspector to identify defects. If they are repaired before the seller puts the house on the market, a higher asking price can be set.

Corey Friedman, of Greater Chicago Home Inspections, inspects a house. Under normal conditions, roof shingles should last for twenty to thirty years. However, other problems, such as holes, moss buildup, and leaks around vent pipes or chimneys, can occur much sooner. Defects such as these can be detected only by careful, up-close inspection.

To carry out an inspection, you must have sound knowledge of home construction and engineering. You'll also need to be physically fit. On a daily basis, you'll be climbing up on roofs, exploring basements, and inspecting attics. No wonder some inspectors joke that their best friend is the folding ladder. Other "friendly" tools include electric outlet testers and moisture meters that identify leaks and seepage.

Tasks such as climbing on roofs and checking electrical wiring obviously present some dangers. Most inspectors at one time or another suffer the odd electrical shock or being singed from the flames of a furnace. When crawling through attics and basements, it is not uncommon to encounter dirt and grime, broken glass, bugs, rodents (living and dead), and additional unpleasant surprises.

Other risks are of a legal nature. Sometimes, even the most careful inspection fails to identify a major defect. Some problems—such as leaks that only occur when the wind blows heavy rain at a certain angle—are almost impossible to foresee during an inspection. When problems like these show up after the house has been purchased, new owners may feel cheated and angry even though an inspection is not a guarantee. Some owners might even consider lawsuits against inspectors. For this reason, many home inspectors have liability insurance to protect themselves from expensive legal battles. The threat of such legal risks also explains why most inspectors work as independent contractors. Inspection firms are cautious about hiring permanent workers and having to carry the blame for their oversights. In an attempt to protect themselves, the firms tend to subcontract inspection work on an individual basis. Nonetheless, running your own inspection business requires little start-up money or equipment and you get to be your own boss.

Since you will need to drum up your own business, good people skills are essential. Home inspectors are usually recommended to buyers by real estate agents, builders, and architects. Buyers will often accompany you on inspections, which usually take between two and three hours. During this time, you will need to outline the home's features in order to educate buyers about the condition of the home.

Following the inspection, you will need to write up a detailed report that will help buyers decide whether to go ahead with the purchase, renegotiate the price of the house, or back out of a bad deal. Although official report forms are available, the ability to write clearly and concisely is important. It is considered unethical to discuss your observations with sellers or real estate agents.

Education and Training

There are no official requirements or education necessary to become a professional home inspector. However, courses taken at technical schools or continuing-education programs can be useful in order to understand electrical, heating, and cooling systems. Math is important for calculations and English composition for writing reports.

Working part-time during the summer for a company that specializes in house construction or renovation can provide you with valuable experience and help you to understand

Home inspectors get down on their knees and use flashlights to inspect furnaces, which are usually located in dark, often dirty basements. During an inspection, the inspector will assess the furnace's age, how well it heats a home or building, and whether it possesses any defects or presents hazardous conditions.

structural and technical aspects of home construction. Other useful jobs include working for an architecture or engineering firm or for an electrician or plumber. Getting an internship (paid or unpaid) at a home inspection company where you can observe an inspector at work is an ideal apprenticeship. Increasingly, technical schools, community colleges, and some online courses are available in home inspection.

Home inspection is not a regulated profession, which means that inspectors don't have to pass any tests or become certified. Nonetheless, in light of the serious consequences of a poor inspection and the competitiveness of the field, increasing numbers of inspectors seek certification from home inspection associations. Associations such as the National Association of Certified Home Inspectors (NACHI) and the American Society of Home Inspectors (ASHI) offer part-time courses and workshops that deal with all aspects of inspection. After gaining some on-the-job experience and passing exams, successful candidates are recognized as certified professionals.

Salary

Home inspection does not always provide steady work. When the housing market is booming, inspectors may carry out three to four inspections a day during a six-day week. However, in slow seasons, competition increases and work can diminish by up to 50 percent. Most inspectors charge by the job, with fees based on the selling price of the house and its square footage. On average, inspectors in North America earn between $250 and $350 per inspection. Certified professionals who offer more experience and additional services—for example, inspections of swimming pools, wells, and septic systems; and testing for radon, asbestos, lead paint fumes, and termites—can compete for more jobs and earn more money. Although some inspectors make around $20,000 a year, others can make up to $70,000.

Outlook

The ASHI estimates that 77 percent of homes sold in the United States and Canada are inspected before they are purchased. This means that there is still opportunity for considerable growth in the field. Furthermore, home inspectors interested in branching out can expand their expertise to include inspections of commercial buildings.

FOR MORE INFORMATION

ORGANIZATIONS

America Institute of Inspectors (AII)
1421 Esplanade Avenue, Suite 7
Klamath Falls, OR 97601
(800) 877-4770
Web site: http://www.inspection.org
  This home inspection association offers training and certification programs for residential and commercial building inspectors.

American Society of Home Inspectors (ASHI)
932 Lee Street, Suite 101
Des Plaines, IL 60016
(800) 743-ASHI (2744)
Web site: http://www.ashi.org

This association for home buyers and sellers, real estate agents, and home inspectors is a good source for education information, inspection standards, and job opportunities. The Web site includes a virtual home inspection tour and an online store that sells inspection tools.

Association of Construction Inspectors
1224 North Nokomis NE
Alexandria, MN 56308
(320) 763-7525
Web site: http://www.iami.org/aci.cfm
This is North America's largest professional organization for people involved in construction inspection and management. The site includes information about professional standards, inspection guidelines, and training and jobs.

Canadian Association of Home Inspectors (CAHI)
P.O. Box 507
64 Reddick Road
Brighton, ON K0K 1H0
Canada
(888) 748-2244 or (613) 475-5699
Web site: http://www.cahi.ca
The voice of Canada's home inspection industry, this national association offers information on standards and a nationwide list of inspectors.

National Association of Certified Home Inspectors (NACHI)
P.O. Box 987
Valley Forge, PA 19482-0987
Web site: http://www.nachi.org
This nonprofit organization helps inspectors build and maintain businesses while keeping them up to date with industry news and standards.

BOOKS

Becker, Norman. *The Complete Book of Home Inspection.* 3rd ed. New York, NY: McGraw-Hill Professional, 2002.
This book provides guidelines for evaluating and inspecting property, both inside and out. Included are lots of useful charts and checklists for identifying problems.

Cauldwell, Rex. *Inspecting a House* (For Pros by Pros). Newtown, CT: Taunton Press, 2000.
With twenty years' of experience as a plumber, electrician, building inspector, and licensed contractor, Cauldwell is well qualified to describe the ins and outs of home inspection.

Pompeii, Michael A. *Become a Home Inspector!: A Concise Guide to Starting Up and Operating a Successful Home Inspection Business.* 2nd ed. Fredericksburg, VA: Pompeii Engineers, 2004.
A straightforward and informative guide that is written by an experienced professional.

Spada, Marcia Darvin. *The Home Inspection Book: A Guide for Professionals.* Cincinnati, OH: South-Western Educational Publishing, 2001.
This book describes the home inspection process, as well as how to set up a business. It includes a workbook and study guides.

PERIODICALS

ASHI Reporter
American Society of Home Inspectors (ASHI)
932 Lee Street, Suite 101
Des Plaines, IL 60016
Web site: http://www.ashi.org/inspectors/reporter.asp
This leading industry magazine includes topical information, useful technical articles, and updates concerning changes in building codes.

7

REAL ESTATE AGENT

Real estate agents thrive on finding the perfect home for people who are seeking to rent or purchase an apartment, house, or vacation property. If you love houses, enjoy meeting new people, and have a knack for selling, you will likely take to the dynamic field of real estate.

Description

For many people, buying or selling a home is one of life's biggest decisions. Locating the right property, negotiating a fair price, finding financing, and closing the deal while respecting local and state or provincial property laws can be an overwhelming challenge. For this reason, most people turn to real estate agents and brokers for help.

As a real estate agent, you basically have to know everything about the housing market in your community. This means keeping up with the market value of all types of properties as well as local zoning and tax laws. You'll need to be aware of interest rates—high interest rates make it more difficult to get loans from banks—and learn where clients can seek financing. You also have to be knowledgeable about your community. Clients with small children, for example, will likely look for a home in a low-crime neighborhood that is close to good schools and recreational facilities such as parks and swimming pools. Elderly clients, however, might be more interested in quiet neighborhoods with plenty of nearby conveniences. Working with all sorts of people to meet their needs means you have to be trustworthy, attentive to detail, and a good listener.

More than half of real estate agents are independent workers. They are contracted by a licensed real estate

Real estate agents, if possible, like to show a home without the possessions of the current occupants. Personal items can often be distracting and make it difficult for buyers to imagine their own furniture in the space. Equally important is showing a home that has been thoroughly cleaned, with walls and ceilings freshly painted, and floors newly varnished.

broker—either a small firm or a franchise of a large national company such as Century 21 or Royal LePage. In return for finding properties to sell and then closing the deal between sellers and buyers, the broker pays the agent a portion of the commission earned from the sale of the property. Brokers manage real estate offices, advertise properties, supervise real estate agents, and handle business and administrative details as well as all paperwork. In the meantime, agents track down new properties whose owners will agree to list these homes for sale with the firm. They also locate potential buyers. Before showing homes to possible buyers, agents meet with them to get a sense of what they're looking for and how much they can spend. If the buyer likes a certain home but can't afford it, the agent will help negotiate a good price with the seller as well as help find financing with a bank or mortgage company.

Agents supervise the writing and signing of the contract between the seller and buyer once a sale is made. It is their responsibility to make sure both parties respect the terms of the contract. For instance, if the seller agrees to make repairs, the agent or broker must make sure that they are actually carried out.

Education and Training

You can't work as a real estate agent unless you have a license. For this, you need to be eighteen years old, have a high school diploma, and pass a written exam that tests your knowledge about real estate and property laws. Many licensing associations also require you to complete between thirty and ninety hours of classroom instruction. Local associations that are members of the National Association of Realtors sponsor introductory real estate courses that cover everything from selling techniques to legal concerns.

Many community colleges and junior colleges offer courses in real estate as well as finance, marketing, statistics, and law—all of which are very helpful. Real estate firms usually offer training programs and courses for beginners. Generally, the larger the firm, the more thorough the training program.

The best way to learn about real estate and make contacts is to get a summer job or internship with a real estate firm working as an assistant to agents or brokers. Starting out in the world of real estate is fairly easy. However, becoming a successful agent who makes many sales and high commissions depends on talent, determination, organizational skills, and an outgoing personality.

Salary

Fixed salaries for real estate agents are low or nonexistent. The main source of income for both real estate agents and brokers is the commission that they make on sales. A commission is a percentage rate of the overall price paid for the home. The rate varies according to the type of property, its value, and what the agent and broker agreed upon. Commissions are often divided between several agents and brokers. The broker or agent that obtained the listing usually splits the commission with the agent who made the sale. The real estate firm that employs them also receives a share, usually about half of the total commission.

As a new agent, it may take weeks or months before you make your first sale. However, with more experience and clients, you can begin making some serious money. Most

A real estate agent for the broker Re/Max sets out a sign advertising homes for sale in Cornelius, Oregon. Usually fully furnished, a model home is a sample house that allows buyers to view the quality and style of all the similar houses that will be built in a residential development. Once all homes have been built and sold, model homes are also sold as residences.

salaried real estate agents make between $20,000 and $53,000 a year, including commissions. The top 10 percent make over $80,000. The challenge of making good money can be a strong motivating force for many real estate agents.

Outlook

Job opportunities for real estate agents are expected to grow slowly over the next decade. In large part, this is due to technological advances. For example, buyers can bypass

The Internet is changing how real estate agents conduct business. Both buyers and agents can save time and energy by doing initial property searches over the Internet and viewing photos, floor plans, and guided video tours. Furthermore, agents with their own Web sites can attract people who want to sell property and buyers from all over the country who are interested in their listings.

certain steps by simply checking out properties and prices on the Internet. Using a computer, an agent can, initially, show clients all of a home's features without having to leave the office. The widespread use of cell phones with Internet access has made it easier for agents to share and trade information with buyers, sellers, lawyers, and contractors much more efficiently. Less time is spent driving around from house to house. In fact, many agents don't even need to work at an office; they can work comfortably out of their own homes. With individual agents able to take on a larger number of clients, competition is tougher for newcomers.

However, buyers depend on agents to handle complex transactions such as the closing of the actual sale. Furthermore, as North Americans continue to view real estate as a secure investment, there will undoubtedly be an increase in property purchases, particularly in cities and in new, suburban areas.

FOR MORE INFORMATION

ORGANIZATIONS
Dearborn Real Estate Education
30 S. Wacker Drive, Suite 2500
Chicago, IL 60606
(800) 621-9621
Web site: http://www.dearborn.com/recampus/reechome.asp
> The nation's top provider of real estate education publishes training materials that are available in print, via software, and online.

National Association of Exclusive Buyer Agents
541 S. Orlando Avenue, Suite 300
Maitland, FL 32751
(800) 986-2322
Web site: http://www.naeba.org
> Buyer Agents work exclusively with buyers to help them locate, finance, inspect, and purchase the ideal property. Their referral Web site offers lists of exclusive buyer agents.

National Association of Realtors
430 North Michigan Avenue
Chicago, IL 60611-4087
(800) 874-6500
Web site: http://www.realtor.org
> The United States' leading organization for realtors offers a wealth of information concerning every aspect of worldwide real estate. The Web site includes news reports, industry research, and information about education and events.

Real Estate Institute of Canada
5407 Eglinton Avenue W., Suite 208
Toronto, ON M9C 5K6
Canada
(416) 695-9000
Web site: http://www.reic.ca
> This association educates and certifies Canadian real estate professionals, and creates networking opportunities between agents and brokers.

WEB SITES

Real-Estate-Agents.com
http://real-estate-agents.com
> A comprehensive directory of real estate agents throughout Canada and the United States.

BOOKS

Cook, Frank. *21 Things I Wish My Broker Had Told Me: Practical Advice for New Real Estate Professionals*. Chicago, IL: Dearborn Real Estate Education, 2002.
> This book of advice features lots of anecdotes, some of them quite humorous, from successful real estate professionals.

Edwards, Kenneth W. *Your Successful Real Estate Career.* 4th ed. New York, NY: American Management Association, 2003.
A comprehensive guide for anyone looking into a real estate career, this book deals with everything from getting a license to succeeding in a highly competitive business.

Foster, Gerald L. *American Houses: A Field Guide to the Architecture of the Home.* Boston, MA: Houghton-Mifflin, 2004.
A thorough and well-illustrated overview of a great variety of American architectural styles ranging from traditional colonial to innovative twentieth century. Great reading for understanding architectural styles and terms.

Kennedy, Danielle, and Warren Jamison. *How to List and Sell Real Estate in the 21st Century.* Upper Saddle River, NJ: Pearson, 1999.
Kennedy is a successful broker who shares techniques for embarking upon a career in real estate. The book includes many tips and anecdotes.

Sullivan, Marilyn. *The Complete Idiot's Guide to Success as a Real Estate Agent.* Indianapolis, IN: Alpha Books, 2003.
This book offers step-by-step advice for people who want to get started in the real estate business. It includes examples of seller and buyer transactions and tips on how to conduct an open house.

PERIODICALS

Realtor
National Association of Realtors
430 North Michigan Avenue
Chicago, IL 60611-4087
Web site: http://www.realtor.org/rmodaily.nsf?OpenDatabase
A print and online magazine from North America's leading real estate association. It includes articles, interviews, business tips, and selling techniques. The online version features exclusive reviews, columns, and resources.

8

HOME PEST CONTROLLER

Think back to last summer's backyard barbecues. Remember how, aside from your friends and family, there were also a lot of annoying bugs present? Well, other North Americans are equally irritated by these and other bothersome, destructive, and sometimes even dangerous pests. This makes getting rid of them not only a pleasure, but also a growing career opportunity.

Description

Pests are more than just annoying. They sting and bite, can spread diseases, and can damage and destroy furniture and homes. Cockroaches, rats, mice, termites, fleas, ants, bees, wasps, and bedbugs are all common pests that infest North American homes, regardless of whether they are tiny rural cabins or elegant urban penthouses. To get rid of these pests, homeowners are giving up on the cheap, often ineffective, remedies sold at retail stores. Instead, they rely increasingly on the services of pest controllers.

As a pest controller, you must know how to locate and identify pests before destroying them. To do this, you'll need to know about their habitats and habits. You'll also have to be familiar with various types of pest management techniques. Applying chemical pesticides is the most popular way of getting rid of pests. "Common use" pesticides—available to the public in weak concentrations—are usually used. If the pest problem is severe, however, you might need to use "restricted use" pesticides. Potentially harmful to pest controllers, clients, and the environment, such pesticides are controlled by the Environmental Protection Agency (EPA). You must be cautious when dealing with any kind of

Pest control is like a detective's job where the bad guys are bugs and rodents. The challenge is to track down and identify any pests, and then determine the least harmful way of getting rid of them. For this reason, two top tools are a flashlight (for finding evidence of vermin in cracks and corners) and a bait gun that applies dabs of deadly poison to carefully chosen spots.

chemical. In fact, before you can begin working in this profession, you must undergo training in both health and safety procedures.

Other frequently used pest management techniques include setting traps and operating equipment capable of freezing, burning, or electrocuting pests. In some cases, you might need to construct a physical barrier that prevents them from entering a home or that cuts them off from food supplies. Another common method is to use poisonous baits that destroy the pests or prevent them from reproducing. Increasingly, pest controllers use a variety of these techniques instead of pesticides. Aside from the environmental risks of some pesticides, many pests are becoming more resistant to them over time.

In general, there are three levels of pest controllers that differ based on training and responsibilities: technicians, applicators, and supervisors (although the names vary depending on your state or province). Pest control technicians locate pests and operate traps. They assist applicators by preparing equipment and dealing with customers. They can only apply pesticides when supervised by an applicator.

Applicators, or exterminators, do the same job as technicians. In addition, they are certified by professional associations to use all kinds of pesticides without supervision. Some applicators might specialize in a particular type of pest or service. Termite exterminators often drill holes into homes to get to termites buried deep within wood. To prevent them from reappearing, they might create obstacles by digging holes or trenches around houses. Fumigators control pests by using poisonous gases called fumigants. Before a home is fumigated, it must be completely sealed and evacuated. Other specialties include rodent control and tree and lawn control. No matter what the specialty, a pest controller needs to be in good physical shape to deal with

For serious problems in which pests have burrowed their way into a home's very structure, fumigation is often the best solution. After evacuating all people, pets, plants, and food, the house is sealed closed within a plastic tentlike structure for twenty-four hours. Poisonous gas is pumped into the home, seeping into every nook and cranny and leaving no pest alive.

the bending, crawling, lifting, and other activities that are required by the job.

Pest control supervisors or operators supervise technicians and applicators. Often, they manage or own the pest control firm. They make sure that their workers follow rules and procedures and deal with the business aspects of the company.

Most pest controllers work standard full-time hours, although many also work weekends and evenings. Since pests thrive in warm climates, there are more job opportunities in southern states where summer months are longer and warmer. In fact, close to half of all American pest controllers work in California, Florida, Georgia, North Carolina, Tennessee, and Texas. The downside to working in warm weather is that it can get very hot beneath the protective gloves, suit, and goggles.

Education and Training

In general, all that is required to be a pest controller is a high school diploma. In addition to good interpersonal skills, it is also useful if you have a driver's license.

Since pest controllers deal with dangerous chemicals, they must follow many federal, state, and provincial environmental regulations. In many states and provinces, you can only become a certified pest controller by acquiring job experience and passing an exam. In most cases, the best way to begin is by getting a job at a pest control firm as an apprentice technician. You'll receive on-the-job training and take courses that help you prepare for technician certification. To be certified as an applicator or a supervisor requires further training and more job experience.

Salary

The average hourly wage for a pest control worker in 2004 was $13.60. Most workers make between $10 and $15 an

Michael Bohdan has been a professional pest controller for over twenty years. In his hometown of Plano, Texas, he runs the Pest Shop, a store that sells a wide variety of pest control products. He is also the founder of one of the most unique museums in North America. Located in a corner of Bohdan's store, the Cockroach Hall of Fame features dead roaches dressed up as celebrities, such as "Marilyn Monroach."

hour. The hourly wage for applicators and supervisors is somewhat higher. Supervisors can earn around $20 an hour. Some pest controllers also receive commissions based on the number of jobs they contract.

Outlook

The pest control industry is estimated to grow slightly in the next decade. As homeowners become more reluctant to resort to difficult and less effective do-it-yourself methods, demand for professional pest controllers will increase. As environmental concerns have led to the banning of some pesticides, more sophisticated forms of pest control management will be needed. This increased specialization should lead to more jobs and higher salaries.

FOR MORE INFORMATION

ORGANIZATIONS

National Pest Management Association (NPMA)
9300 Lee Highway, Suite 301
Fairfax, VA 22031
(703) 352-NPMA (6762)
Web site: http://www.pestworld.org
> The national trade association for the professional pest control industry offers educational programs and information about all aspects of pest control for both homeowners and pest controllers.

WEB SITES

Pest Control Technology
http://www.pctonline.com
> This site provides a wealth of pest-related information and has links to products and resources, and an online magazine. News flashes with recent headlines such as "Carpenter Ants Eating U.S. Homes" and "Student Battles Effects of Spider Bite" make for engaging reading.

Pestproducts.com
http://pestproducts.com/index.htm
> This online pest control store offers a variety of professional products and advice.

Pest Web

http://www.pestweb.com

This site bills itself as the pest control industry's leading information center. It includes everything from descriptions of the pests themselves to updates about products and technology. There is also plenty of news, online training courses, and an advice column called "Ask Mr. Pest Control."

BOOKS

Bohdan, Michael. *What's Buggin' You? Michael Bohdan's Guide to Home Pest Control.* Los Angeles, CA: Santa Monica Press, 1998.
Bohdan has over twenty years' experience as a professional pest controller (and is the founder of the Cockroach Hall of Fame). In this practical and humorous guide, he explains how to identify and control a large variety of pests.

Castner, James L. *Photographic Atlas of Entomology and Guide to Insect Identification.* Gainesville, FL: Feline Press, 2000.
Castner spent twenty-five years photographing insects for magazines ranging from *National Geographic* to *Ranger Rick* before publishing this colorful insect identification guide.

Cranshaw, Whitney. *Garden Insects of North America: The Ultimate Guide to Backyard Bugs* (Princeton Field Guides). Princeton, NJ: Princeton University Press, 2004.
North America boasts more than 100,000 species of insects and related garden pests. Cranshaw identifies most of them. This book is organized according to what type of damage they inflict on homes and gardens, and includes methods of pest control as well as discussions of insects that can be beneficial to humans.

Kramer, Richard. *PCT Technician's Handbook: A Guide to Pest Identification and Management.* 3rd ed. Cleveland, OH: Pest Control Technology, 1998.
This guide is a very thorough and useful resource for professional pest controllers.

Olkowski, William, Sheila Daar, and Helga Olkowski. *Common-Sense Pest Control: Least-Toxic Solutions for Your Home, Garden, Pets and Community.* Newtown, CT: Taunton Press, 1991.
    The authors founded the Bio-Integral Resource Center in Berkeley, California, which is dedicated to nontoxic pest management. The book discusses everything you need to know about pests and environmentally friendly ways of dealing with them.
Stein, Dan. *Least Toxic Home Pest Control.* Summertown, TN: Book Publishing Company, 1994.
    This practical guide mixes humor and common sense while exploring ways of outsmarting pests without resorting to chemicals.
Van Emden, H. F., and M. W. Service. *Pest and Vector Control.* New York, NY: Cambridge University Press, 2004.
    In this large academic book, two leading entomologists (bug specialists) discuss various ways of controlling pests without harming humans and the environment.

9

HOME APPLIANCE REPAIRER

When you were younger, did you enjoy taking apart your toys and gadgets and putting (or trying to put) them back together again? Were you fascinated by how the appliances in your home worked? If you still like mechanical challenges, you might want to consider solving them for a living—as a home appliance repairer.

Description

A home is not complete without the basic appliances we have come to rely upon: refrigerators, freezers, stoves, microwaves, washers and dryers, air conditioners, and vacuum cleaners. When one of them breaks down and we suddenly find ourselves unable to cook our food or wash our clothes, we realize how important it is to have a fast, reliable, and efficient home appliance repairer.

When a machine starts leaking or making strange noises, or if it stops functioning altogether, it is time to call a home appliance repairer. There is usually a difference between specialists who repair small appliances and those who tackle large ones. In general, small-appliance repairers are trained to fix various portable items, ranging from microwaves to blenders. They usually work out of their own shops. Meanwhile, those who work on large, more complex appliances—such as refrigerators and dishwashers—tend to specialize in only one or two appliances. Because of the size of these appliances, they make house calls.

As a home appliance repairer, the first thing you'll do upon arriving at a client's home will be to check for clues—loose parts, leaks, odd noises, signs of rust or wear—to determine what is wrong. Aside from your knowledge of specific appliances, you may need to consult service manuals to figure out the exact problem and how to fix it. You might have to take the appliance apart to check inner mechanisms such as wiring and electronics systems. Equipment such as voltmeters and wattmeters are used to test these systems for flaws.

Faulty parts such as gears, switches, belts, motors, and electronic circuit boards must be repaired or replaced. Before reassembling the appliance, you will need to clean, oil, and tighten all parts, so that the appliance will be in perfect operating condition. You will have to exercise extreme caution with refrigerators and air conditioners because of the chemical refrigerants used to cool these appliances. Potentially dangerous to people and the environment, refrigerants have to be treated and disposed of with great care. Other potential job hazards include electrical shocks and muscle sprains from lifting heavy objects.

A repairer is nothing without his or her tool kit. This includes wrenches, pliers, and screwdrivers as well as more specialized tools such as soldering guns and electrical

> Many things can go wrong with a washing machine. It can refuse to spin, drain, or fill with water; it can leak, make noises, or fail to advance from one cycle to another; or it can simply stop working altogether. Whatever the problem may be, to avoid injury or even death, a repairer should always disconnect an appliance from its power source before attempting any investigative or repair work.

equipment. In your truck or van (you can't be a large-appliance repairer without a driver's license), you should have a stock of spare parts, too. Repairers who do house calls usually service four or five homes in a day. Aside from regular service calls, you'll have to deal with emergencies in which appliances are leaking dangerous fluids or gas. Most repairers work standard daytime hours, although some may work overtime and on weekends.

Although some repairers have their own small businesses and repair shops, many work for retailers such as home and electronic appliance stores and department stores. When a customer purchases a new appliance, such as a refrigerator or washing machine, a home appliance service person is in charge of delivering the new product, installing it, and showing the owner how to safely operate it.

If you work for a large repair shop or service center, with time you may work your way up to supervisor, parts manager, or service manager. Along with technical know-how, you will need to have good interpersonal skills for these managerial positions.

Education and Training

In most cases, home appliance repairers must have a high school diploma. As a repairer, you will need to be able to read instruction manuals (usually in English) and follow diagrams. Training usually takes place on the job. You will

Maytag repairman Robert Yon removes tools from his van as he prepares to make a service call in Tyrone, Georgia. As sales of appliances in North America have decreased, there has been an increased demand for repair services. Responding to this trend, Maytag, a leading manufacturer of washers, dryers, refrigerators, and dishwashers, trains its repairers to service appliances made by other top brands, such as Whirlpool, Kenmore, Frigidaire, and General Electric.

probably start off by learning all there is to know about one type of appliance before mastering another. A part-time or summer job repairing appliances or any kind of mechanical or electronics equipment can provide you with valuable experience. Familiarity with basic electronics is increasingly important because more appliances are manufactured with electronic (as opposed to manual) control systems.

Since larger appliances are more complex, repairers of this equipment often take specialized training courses at a trade school or community college. Many employers seek job candidates who have completed one- or two-year training programs at vocational high schools or community colleges. Large-appliance makers, such as Whirlpool and Maytag, often provide their own training programs to their employees and repairers who regularly sell and service their appliances. Manufacturers frequently offer workshops and seminars to keep repairers up to date with new technology.

Although it is not necessary, becoming a certified home appliance repairer will improve your job prospects. Numerous associations, including the International Society of Certified Electronics Technicians (ISCET) and the Professional Service Association (PSA), offer certification training programs. You must receive EPA (Environmental Protection Agency) certification to repair refrigerators.

Salary

In 2004, the average income for a home appliance repairer, including commission (some repairers also earn commission based on the number of appliances they fix in one day), was around $33,500 a year. Repairers who are starting out can expect to earn around $18,000, while those with a few years of experience can earn close to $50,000. Earnings vary depending on the region and the amount of skill and knowledge required to fix a certain appliance.

Outlook

As appliances become more technologically sophisticated, home owners will increasingly require the services of skilled repairers. As a result, manufacturers, dealers, and large chain stores will need to train employees and hire new ones so they understand these new features and technology. Without access to this knowledge, small repair shops and self-employed repairers will find it increasingly difficult to stay in business.

FOR MORE INFORMATION

ORGANIZATIONS

International Society of Certified Electronics Technicians (ISCET)
3608 Pershing Avenue
Fort Worth, TX 76107-4527
(800) 946-0201 or (817) 921-9101
Web site: http://www.iscet.org

ISCET runs education and training programs that certify technicians in the electronics and appliance service industry. The Web site includes an online store and career center.

National Appliance Service Association (NASA)
P.O. Box 2514
Kokomo, IN 46904
(765) 453-1820
Web site: http://www.nasa1.org

Includes information from experts about the service and sales of small appliances.

North American Retail Dealers Association
10 E. 22nd Street, Suite 310
Lombard, IL 60148
(800) 621-0298 or (630) 953-8950
Web site: http://www.narda.com/
> This nonprofit trade association represents independent retailers that sell and service all types of consumer home products. It offers information about education and training programs and provides business services.

United Servicers Association
6428 Coldwater Canyon Avenue
North Hollywood, CA 91606
(800) 683-2558
Web site: http://www.unitedservicers.com
> An organization run by service people dedicated to helping professional repairers operate successful businesses in Canada and the United States.

WEB SITES

Appliance University
http://www.applianceuniversity.com
> This Web site bills itself as the number-one source for major appliance service training information.

Professional Service Association (PSA)
http://www.psaworld.com/main.html
> This site provides industry news, business information, and other helpful resources for independent service professionals.

BOOKS

Davidson, Homer L. *TV Repair for Beginners.* 5th ed. New York, NY: McGraw-Hill, 1998.

Whether you want to become a well-paid TV repairer or want to keep your set out of the repair shop, this thorough guide will help.

Dixon, Graham. *Electrical Appliances: The Complete Step-by-Step Guide to the Repair and Maintenance of a Wide Range of Domestic Electrical Appliances*. 3rd ed. Somerset, England: Haynes Publishing, 1995.
An illustrated guide to repairing numerous home appliances.

Kleinert, Eric. *Troubleshooting and Repairing Major Appliances*. New York, NY: McGraw-Hill, 1995.
A useful reference book for on-the-job repairs that covers everything electricians and apprentices need to know.

Langley, Billy C. *Major Appliances: Operation, Maintenance, Troubleshooting, and Repair*. Englewood Cliffs, NJ: Prentice Hall, 1993.
This book provides a basic introduction to major appliances used in most residences as well as how to service them.

Maxwell, Lee. *Save Women's Lives: History of Washing Machines*. Eaton, CO: Oldewash, 2003.
Maxwell is a retired professor of electrical engineering who has collected and restored 1,000 antique washing machines and built the world's only washing machine museum. In this book, he provides a history of washing machines and describes tracking down and restoring the items in his collection.

Wood, Robert. *All Thumbs Guide to Repairing Major Home Appliances*. Blue Ridge Summit, PA: TAB Books, 1992.
This book includes instructions on how to repair major home appliances and is accompanied by detailed illustrations.

RESIDENTIAL LANDSCAPER

Many home owners will tell you that a home isn't complete without a garden. Even residents of condominium complexes and apartment buildings pay increasing attention to the landscaping possibilities of courtyards, terraces, driveways, and rooftops. Arranging a garden's elements—from trees, shrubs, and flowers to footpaths, decks, fences, and lighting—is the job of a landscaper. If you're creative, like nature, and love to spend time outside, you might consider becoming a residential landscaper.

Description

Landscape workers are involved in producing and maintaining a home's exterior spaces. Although landscapers only infrequently create these spaces—planning and design is usually done by certified landscape architects with four-year specialized degrees—they are in charge of making sure exteriors stay both functional and beautiful. This involves planting, trimming, and tending to flowers, shrubs, and trees to keep them attractive and healthy. Transporting and spreading soil, mulch, fertilizers, and pesticides are performed on a seasonal basis. Other gardening duties include seeding, fertilizing, watering, and mowing lawns. It is important to know about different types of plants and flowers, their needs, and the best growing conditions.

Although most people think landscaping deals primarily with gardens, landscape workers often tackle a variety of other projects. These could include leveling sloped land; building brick walls; constructing wooden fences; or laying paths of wood, tile, or ornamental stones. Installing outdoor lights; setting up a sprinkler system; and building a fountain, deck, or veranda are also common landscaping jobs.

As you can imagine, most of this work involves a fair amount of physical effort. Since you will be required to do a lot of lifting, climbing, digging, bending, and carrying, you will need to be in good physical shape. You will use motorized equipment such as minitractors, mowers, hedge trimmers, and chain saws, as well as manual tools such as shovels, rakes, hoes, hand saws, shears, and clippers. Exposure to extreme temperatures, annoying insects, and the odd thorn or splinter are also part of being a landscaper.

Although many landscapers work all year round, the types of jobs performed change with the seasons. For example, in autumn you'll rake and clear dead leaves and branches, and in the winter you'll need to cover plants and shovel snow. In the springtime, you'll be busy clearing debris and planting new bulbs and seeds. Different climates mean that landscaping tasks will be done during different times of the year depending on if you're working in southern Canada and the northern United States or in regions such as Florida, California, and Arizona, where it is usually warm throughout the year.

Around a quarter of all landscape workers are self-employed. They either work on their own or, depending on the size of a job, with a partner or small team of workers on a project-to-project basis. As a self-employed landscaper, you have to be good at advertising your services. You'll need to be determined in seeking out new projects and clients. Many landscape workers, however, prefer to work on a contract basis for large landscape firms. With time, you can work your way up to a supervisory position. Supervisors manage workers and the financial aspects of a

A variety of tools are used by a tree and landscape service in Victorville, California. Common equipment for landscapers ranges from hand tools such as shovels, rakes, and pruning shears to power machinery such as chain saws, hedge and weed trimmers, mowers, and rototillers (machines whose metal blades turn over the soil in preparation for planting).

project such as the costs of materials, tools, and labor. Taking into account the client's budget, they are also responsible for making sure that the final result meets with the client's satisfaction.

Education and Training

No formal education is required to be a landscaper. Some vocational high schools offer courses in landscaping or

The two landscapers seen here are planting a decorative border of flowers and plants along the top of a stone wall. This border is a type of informal garden and is relatively easy to care for. The plants grow as they would in the wild and do not need to be pruned to precise heights or shapes.

gardening, as do community colleges and private gardening associations. However, the simplest way to gain some initial experience as a landscaper is to work, whether paid or as a volunteer, in your own garden or in the garden of a relative or neighbor. Many small landscaping firms contract students for seasonal help, particularly in the spring and summer. City parks also routinely hire students for summer jobs as groundskeepers, as do hotels and resorts, golf courses, and botanical gardens. Such jobs provide you with experience and important contacts. Specialized landscaping courses at a junior or agricultural college can prepare you for your own landscaping business or a career as a freelance landscape designer.

Once you have a certain amount of work experience and training, you can pass a written exam that will make you a certified landscaper. Various professional organizations, such as PLANET (the Professional Landcare Network), offer this certification. Although not necessary, certification gives you an edge in obtaining jobs and earning more money.

Salary

According to the U.S. Bureau of Labor Statistics, in 2004, landscape workers earned an average of $10.70 an hour. Supervisors at landscaping companies earned close to $16. Depending on how often landscapers work and their degree of experience, they can earn between $23,000 and $60,000 a year, although managers of large firms or successful entrepreneurs can earn more.

Outlook

Opportunities for landscapers are expected to increase over the next decade. The combination of low earnings and tiring physical labor results in frequent job turnover. As a result, landscaping firms are often looking for new workers.

Meanwhile, most busy home owners have full-time jobs and less opportunity to take care of their gardens. At the same time, they are placing increasing importance on the environment in general and on their own exteriors as spaces for relaxation and leisure. In fact, home owners are entertaining in their yards and on their decks more than ever before. Furthermore, people selling their homes have discovered that well-kept gardens add to the value of one's property. For all of these reasons, home owners will increasingly turn to landscapers to create and maintain their grounds and gardens.

FOR MORE INFORMATION

ORGANIZATIONS

American Nursery and Landscape Association
1000 Vermont Avenue NW, Suite 300
Washington, DC 20005
(202) 789-2900
Web site: http://www.anla.org
This association provides education, research, and public-relations services to planters, retailers, designers, and landscapers.

Canadian Nursery Landscape Association (CNLA)
RR #4, Station Main
7856 Fifth Street
Milton, ON L9T 2X8
Canada

(905) 875-1399

Web site: http://www.canadanursery.com/canadanursery/index.lasso
   The CNLA brings together provincial associations representing the
   landscape, horticulture, and nursery industries across Canada. It
   offers educational programs and provides information about new
   trends, landscaping events, and jobs.

Professional Landcare Network (PLANET)

950 Herndon Parkway, Suite 450

Herndon, VA 20170

(800) 395-2522 or (703) 736-9666

Web site: http://www.landcarenetwork.org
   PLANET is a recent amalgamation of Associated Landscape
   Contractors of America (ALCA) and the Professional Lawn Care
   Association of America (PLCAA). An international association, it
   promotes an exchange of business and technical ideas for land-
   scapers who want to create and operate businesses.

WEB SITES

Better Homes and Gardens

http://www.bhg.com/bhg/gardening/index.jhtml
   This useful site includes photos of stunning gardens, a plant data-
   base, information on tools, and advice from experts.

Career Connections Training Centre

http://www.career-connections.bc.ca/garden.htm
   This useful Canadian site for people interested in landscaping
   careers offers information about education and training programs,
   work experience, and job placement assistance.

Landscape Online

http://www.landscapeonline.com
   A top landscape industry site that offers a wide range of information concerning landscape trends, products, and jobs.

Progardenbiz.com
http://www.progardenbiz.com
This online magazine for professional gardeners and landscape contractors provides helpful articles as well as tips and techniques related to gardening.

BOOKS

Better Homes and Gardens, eds. *New Complete Guide to Landscaping: Design, Plant, Build.* 2nd ed. Des Moines, IA: Better Homes and Gardens, 2002.
This easy-to-follow guide outlines how to plan and build a range of basic landscape projects.

Brickell, Christopher, ed. *American Horticultural Society Encyclopedia of Gardening.* New York, NY: DK Adult, 2003.
For amateurs and experts, this gardening bible is written in a friendly, informative style.

Buchanan, Rita. *Taylor's Master Guide to Landscaping.* Boston, MA: Houghton Mifflin, 2000.
A practical yet creative guide about how to landscape small- to medium-sized home gardens.

Dell, Owen E. *How to Start a Home-Based Landscaping Business.* 2nd ed. Guilford, CT: Globe Pequot Press, 1997.
A detailed guide that describes how to set up and successfully operate a landscaping business from your own home.

Von Trapp, Sara Jane. *Landscaping from the Ground Up.* Newtown, CT: Taunton Press, 1997.
Everything you need to know about how to plan and carry out major or minor residential landscape work.

White, Lee Anne, ed. *Landscaping Your Home: Creative Ideas from America's Best Gardeners.* Newtown, CT: Taunton Press, 2001.
This collection of informative articles by expert gardeners and landscapers illustrates how to provide complete yard makeovers.

PERIODICALS

Garden Design

460 N. Orlando Avenue, Suite 200
Winter Park, FL 32789
Web site: http://www.gardendesignmag.com/index.jsp
  A magazine for design-conscious readers who enjoy the outdoors
  and appreciate a well-designed garden.

Landscape Management

7500 Old Oak Boulevard
Cleveland, OH 44130
(440) 891-2729
Web site: http://www.landscapemanagement.net
  A magazine that provides news about gardening industry issues
  and all aspects of landscaping.

Lawn & Landscape

4012 Bridge Avenue
Cleveland, OH 44113
(800) 456-0707
Web site: http://www.lawnandlandscape.com
  Articles on everything from trees, weeds, seeds, blowers, and
  ornaments to how to manage your own business.

11

PROFESSIONAL ORGANIZER

Do you ever think that life seems to be getting increasingly hectic? With many adults working longer hours and accumulating and consuming more, their homes can get quite cluttered. It's hard to get things done, let alone unwind, in a chaotic home. And for the growing number of people who work from home, a messy house can seriously hamper productivity. Instead of drowning in the stress of mess, more and more busy and desperate people are turning to professional organizers, or POs, to organize and simplify their lives. If you're a natural-born neat freak, you might want to consider transforming your tidiness into a career.

Description

Being a successful PO involves more than simply getting clients to clean up clutter and throw things away. You'll need to use a combination of experience and sensitivity to design an organizing system that is in sync with each client's personality. Your first step will be an at-home consultation to get to know clients and their homes and identify problems and goals. In order for your clients to develop new organization habits, you'll have to figure out why a person can't stand throwing out a closet full of clothes or keeping a room clean. Based on what clients want and how much money they can spend, you can then propose a plan of action that will probably involve some of the following:

- deciding what is unnecessary and getting rid of it (not just throwing it in the garbage, but storing, recycling, selling, or giving it away)
- reorganizing and rearranging objects and furniture for more space
- creating or acquiring storage solutions—ranging from shelving units and cupboards to baskets, containers, filing systems, and bulletin boards

- redecorating—different colors, furniture, and lighting can create a more comfortable and efficient space
- creating a list of new organizational routines and habits to prevent clutter and mess from returning

You need little or no money to start up your own PO business, but you will need to have some basic business skills in order to control costs and create a successful marketing plan. You'll also need to be aware of the latest organizing trends and products available on the market.

Although many professional organizers work strictly as consultants, others give workshops or write books, articles, and newsletters about organizing. Some also create and/or sell organizational products. There are even residential POs who specialize in certain services and solutions such as organizing home offices, libraries, closets, children's rooms, kitchens, and garages. Others cater to certain types of clients, such as seniors or people with disabilities.

As these before and after photos show, professional organizers can make an enormous difference in people's lives. POs believe that clutter can be an obstacle to success and well-being, and therefore try to find out the emotional reasons behind why clients can't part with possessions. Once clients understand their motivations for hoarding, they discover that letting go of their belongings can be liberating, leaving them with spaces that are more functional and relaxing.

Q & A with a Working Pro

Hellen Buttigieg is a professional organizer, a life coach, the TV host of *Neat*, and founder of We Organize U in Oakville, Canada:

Q: HOW DID YOU DECIDE TO BECOME A PROFESSIONAL ORGANIZER?

A: I saw an article in a local newspaper about someone who organizes homes for a living and instantly knew it was for me. I joined Professional Organizers in Canada (POC) and signed up to be on the board at the first meeting I attended.

Q: HAVE YOU ALWAYS BEEN A NEAT/ORGANIZED PERSON YOURSELF? WHAT WAS YOUR ROOM LIKE WHEN YOU WERE GROWING UP?

A: Although not all professional organizers were neat as kids, I was always highly organized. My parents never had to ask me to clean my room! I realized from a young age that I felt better in a tidy room and I could get more accomplished if my space was organized. Not only was my room always tidy, every drawer had clothes neatly folded and every paper was filed alphabetically.

Q: HOW DO YOU FIND CLIENTS AND KEEP YOURSELF BUSY ENOUGH TO MAKE A LIVING?

A: Most of my clients now see me on the show Neat *and contact me by phone or e-mail. Before I had the TV show, I attracted clients through my Web site, by being listed on several online directories, and by conducting organizing seminars for various groups. It takes time to build a clientele and begin to make a living, but if you want it badly enough and believe in your business, it can be done. Overcoming the fear of putting yourself out there is the hardest part.*

Q: WHAT'S THE MOST EXTREME CLUTTER SITUATION YOU'VE EVER ENCOUNTERED?

A: I see extreme clutter situations quite a bit. The most extreme was a large family home where I had to clear clutter just to get into the front door and up the staircase; it was a safety hazard to live there.

Q: WHAT'S THE HARDEST PART OF YOUR JOB?

A: It can be draining, both physically and emotionally, so it's crucial that I make self-care a priority in order to be fully present for my clients.

Q: WHAT'S THE MOST REWARDING PART?

A: The most rewarding part of my job is having the opportunity to inspire, motivate, and give people the tools to help change their lives. Practically overnight, I see people move from feeling overwhelmed and hopeless to feeling confident and in control of their lives. It's also very fulfilling to use my natural talents and abilities to make a living.

Hellen Buttigieg helps a client sort through an avalanche of toys for an episode of her television show, *Neat*. Buttigieg doesn't just clear up clutter and walk away. She considers clients' natures and habits and then creates organizing solutions that they can stick to. She also invites clients to keep in touch by e-mail to let her know how the new systems are working for them.

Education and Training

Although there are no official manuals or educational programs for becoming a professional organizer, there are many useful books and Web sites. The National Association of Professional Organizers (NAPO) can put you in touch with practicing POs near you who can act as mentors or coaches. Many POs offer workshops and classes at community colleges. You may be able to work with them as an apprentice or assistant. By 2007, NAPO plans to have a certification program in operation that will include specific educational standards and offerings.

Salary

How much you earn depends on how much business you can drum up. Professional organizers who are starting out earn anywhere between $35 and $50 an hour. Some POs prefer to charge a flat fee for each project. There is usually a difference in price for whether you are simply consulting with clients or doing hands-on organizing work. You can supplement your income by giving seminars and workshops and writing self-help books.

Outlook

Professional organizing is an expanding field because people are becoming busier and POs are becoming increasingly specialized. Although the competition is growing (thanks, in part, to the popularity of makeover TV shows), smart and ambitious people who know how to design and market their own unique services can make a good living as organizers.

FOR MORE INFORMATION

ORGANIZATIONS

Julie Morgenstern's Professional Organizers
850 7th Avenue, Suite 901
New York, NY 10019
1-86-ORGANISE (866-742-6473) or (212) 544-8722
Web site: http://www.juliemorgenstern.com
Organizing expert Julie Morgenstern's work has been featured on *Oprah*, the *Today* show, and in the *New York Times*. Her Web site offers tips, products, idea exchanges, and before and after photos as well as information about workshops and getting started as a PO.

National Association of Professional Organizers (NAPO)
4700 W. Lake Avenue
Glenview, IL 60025
(847) 375-4746
Web site: http://www.napo.net
NAPO is North America's leading PO association, with information and research about every aspect of this growing industry. Members include organizers, speakers, trainers, and authors.

Professional Organizers in Canada
255 Dundas Street West
P.O. Box 82032
Waterdown, ON L0R 2M0
Canada
(403) 217-1148
Web site: http://www.organizersincanada.com
This association of professional organizers throughout Canada offers workshops, conferences, seminars, and member listings. Its Web site contains news and articles about organizing.

WEB SITES

Get Organized Now!
http://www.getorganizednow.com/po.html
> How to start and manage your own professional organizing business. This site features newsletters, tips, interviews, articles, discussion forums, and a directory of professional organizers.

National Study Group on Chronic Disorganization
http://www.nsgcd.org
> An interesting online resource for anyone who is interested (professionally or personally) in chronic disorganization.

Online Organizing.com
http://www.onlineorganizing.com/BecomeAnOrganizer.asp
> A helpful Web site for those interested in or already working as organizers. Aside from publishing newsletters and start-up guides, it offers handy marketing tips, practical advice, and a list of useful links.

Organized-Living.com
http://www.organized-living.com
> A dynamic site with articles, checklists for staying organized, a bookstore, an organizing products cybershop, and links to various training programs.

Professional Organizers' Web Ring
http://www.organizerswebring.com
> A useful site with links to many professional organizers, products, books, articles, and Web sites. Includes a discussion forum with many topics of interest.

Stacks and Stacks
http://www.stacksandstacks.com
> This site lists numerous organizing products for every room in the house including laundry rooms, closets, and garages.

BOOKS

Kolberg, Judith. *Conquering Chronic Disorganization*. Decatur, GA: Squall Press, 1999.
This book, written by the founder of the National Study Group on Chronic Disorganization, offers various techniques for dealing with clutter, storage problems, and time management.

Morgenstern, Julie. *Organizing from the Inside Out: The Foolproof System for Organizing Your Home, Your Office, and Your Life*. 2nd ed. New York, NY: Henry Holt, 2004.
Leading organizing expert Morgenstern writes about overcoming obstacles to get and stay organized.

Morgenstern, Julie. *Organizing from the Inside Out for Teens: The Foolproof System for Organizing Your Room, Your Time, and Your Life*. New York, NY: Henry Holt, 2002.
Morgenstern and her daughter Jessi wrote this book to help teens organize their rooms as well as their lives.

Seidler, Cyndi. *A Manual for Professional Organizers*. Sylmar, CA: Banter Books, 2004.
A practical guide on how to start and operate your own PO business.

Steinbacher, Lisa. *The Professional Organizer's Complete Business Guide*. Newbury Park, CA: Eternity Publishing, 2004.
Advice for starting up and running your own organizing business. The book comes with a CD-ROM of templates you can use to create forms, proposals, and advertising materials.

12

HOME STAGER

When people prepare to sell their house or apartment, the biggest obstacle they encounter is how to stop thinking of their private living space as a home full of personal objects and cherished memories. According to real estate agents, they should be thinking of their home as a product that must attract as many buyers as possible. Because it's

aged Home

Barb Schwarz, the creator of the home staging concept, gives a seminar in Concord, California. Over 500,000 people have taken Schwarz's Accredited Staging Professional (ASP) course, which teaches people how to start and operate a staging business.

often hard for home owners to do this in an objective manner, they are relying increasingly on experts called stagers to do it for them. If you like the idea of using your creative flair to set the stage for prospective home buyers, you might want to investigate this emerging profession.

Description

The term "homestaging" was first used by Barb Schwarz, an interior designer from Seattle, Washington. In 1972, Schwarz became a real estate agent and began consulting with home owners on how they could "stage" their properties to sell them for more money. Schwarz, who founded the International Association of Home Staging Professionals in 2001, advised sellers to think of their homes as a stage set, with buyers as the audience and the stager as the director.

The trick to staging a home is to de-clutter, neutralize, or bland it (common terms used by stagers). In doing so, you remove signs of its owners. Prospective buyers can get distracted by personal mementos like photos and might be turned off by highly personalized design choices such as brilliant purple walls, shag carpeting, enormous plants, or fluorescent lighting. When buyers view a home, they want to be able to visualize their own possessions inside it. They also need to see all of a home's features—from front doors and wooden floors to space—in their best possible light.

As a stager—also known as a fluffer, enhancer, or styler—you'll need to have good organizational skills and a strong sense of design. You also need to have good people skills. You'll work with sellers, helping them store or get rid of clutter, thus transforming their home. Selling, moving, and opening up their homes to strangers is stressful for many people. They may feel defensive about having to get rid of clutter and touchy about suggestions such as hiding cat litter or taking down provocative artwork. It takes a sensitive touch to deal with many sellers and convince them to make over their homes.

Some stagers work for real estate firms as selling agents. Others have their own freelance businesses, marketing their services directly to home owners. Depending on your clients' needs and budgets, you might only give consultations, providing tips on what sellers can do to

As these before and after photos show, in real estate first impressions are critical. Before being staged by a StagedHomes professional, this house was hidden by overgrown trees that gave the property an ill-kept look and prevented sunlight from illuminating the interior. By simply trimming trees and shrubs and adding some outdoor lighting, the house has gained in attractiveness—and value.

improve their home. In other cases, you might be in charge of getting rid of and either buying or renting new furniture; finding storage solutions; cleaning, painting, and redecorating; and even suggesting renovations. If your client owns a house, you'll need to focus on the exterior as well, along with the garage, driveway, yard, surrounding trees, and shrubbery. For this reason, it is important to cultivate good

working relationships with furniture and construction supply retailers, painters, movers, landscapers, and other related tradespeople. Although a radical makeover can be costly—some sellers spend between $5,000 and $15,000 on staging—experts estimate that for every $1 spent, a home's value increases by $1.50. Some sellers are so happy with the transformation that they hire stagers to help decorate when they move into their new homes.

Education and Training

There is no specific education recommended if you want to become a stager. Taking courses or seminars in interior design and real estate sales can be useful. It is also a good idea to read decorating magazines, books, or Web sites and to watch TV programs such as *Neat* in Canada and *Trading Spaces* in the United States. The International Association of Home Staging Professionals runs training programs and workshops with classroom and hands-on courses that give participants a certificate in professional staging.

Salary

Most stagers will work with a homeowner for a day or two. Fees vary according to geographic location and the type of service provided. However, on average, stagers charge between $60 and $85 an hour as a basic consulting fee. Depending on the number of rooms involved, you can earn

Some Tips of the Trade

- **The 50 percent rule:** Clutter is often the number-one problem for stagers. Store, give away, or sell half of the client's accumulated belongings to give a home a spacious, clean look.
- **Neutral colors:** Repainting walls in soothing neutral tones often increases the sense of space, light, and cleanliness of a home.
- **Decor:** Most people have too much furniture, hence some needs to be stored or given away. In the event furniture is old, worn, or mismatched, stagers can buy or rent furniture.
- **Extreme cleaning:** Everything, including curtains and carpets, needs to be professionally and thoroughly cleaned. This gives buyers a sense that the entire house is in tip-top condition.
- **Ambiance:** Many stagers recommend playing low, soothing music, such as jazz, and having fresh-cut flowers and welcoming smells such as scented candles or home-baked cookies.
- **Props:** Accents such as throw pillows, fancy bedding, and extra-fluffy towels are important details.

> - **Storage:** Empty closets and cupboards. Store or get rid of some of the clothes in a closet to make it appear more spacious. Hang clothes on wooden hangers and organize clothes according to color.

between $700 and $3,000 per project. For example, one home stager, who arranged for painting, had columns removed, rearranged furniture, improved the lighting, and brought in accessories such as plants and throw pillows for a two-bedroom Manhattan apartment, charged a fee of $1,600.

Outlook

Popular on the West Coast for over a decade, staging is a new but rapidly growing field, particularly in large urban centers such as New York City and Toronto. As real estate markets continue to grow and more agents and sellers recognize the value of a staged home, there should be more opportunities for those who are interested in this field.

FOR MORE INFORMATION

ORGANIZATIONS

Interior Arrangement and Design Association (IADA)
Box 777
6333 East Mockingbird Lane, Suite 147
Dallas, TX 75214
(214) 826-2474
Web site: http://www.interiorarrangement.org
> The Interior Arrangement and Design Association was created to maintain professional standards in the field of one-day makeovers. IADA offers training and certification.

International Association of Home Staging Professionals
4807 Clayton Road, Suite #100
Concord, CA 94521
(800) 392-7161
Web site: http://stagedhomes.com
> This association offers information and training programs for those who want to become professional stagers. The Web site provides a list of professional stagers and the homes they have staged that are for sale.

WEB SITES

Center Stage Home
http://www.centerstagehome.com
> A Web site that offers consulting and staging services as well as training programs for people who want to become professional home stagers. There are also links to other useful sites, information about workshops, and job offers.

BOOKS

Matzke, Lori. *Home Staging: Creating Buyer-Friendly Rooms to Sell Your House.* Arlington, MN: Center Stage Home, 2004.
A guide to staging with detailed commentary and before and after photos of eight homes that were made over by stager Lori Matzke.

Selinger-Eaton, Peggy, and Gayla Moghannam. *Peggy's Corner: The Art of Staging.* Danville, CA: Eaton-Moghannam, 2004.
This book offers successful techniques for staging homes. It comes with a fifty-minute DVD that follows Selinger-Eaton, a professional stager, at work as she transforms average homes into buyers' dreams.

Zackheim, Sarah Parsons, and Martha Webb. *Dress Your House for Success: 5 Fast, Easy Steps to Selling Your House, Apartment, or Condo for the Highest Possible Price!* New York, NY: Three Rivers Press, 1997.
Simple techniques for stagers or homeowners who want to increase the value of a home.

GLOSSARY

apprentice Someone who learns the basics of a job by working under the supervision of a professional.

asbestos A mineral used for fireproofing, for insulation, and as a building material; if inhaled over long periods of time, it can cause cancer.

autonomous Functioning independently without control of others.

bland Tranquil, inoffensive, lacking distinct flavor.

broker Someone who acts as an agent for others, by negotiating contracts, purchases, or sales in return for a fee or commission.

contractor Someone who agrees to furnish materials or perform services for a specified price.

ergonomics The science of using information about human beings to design efficient spaces suitable for their needs.

fluctuate To change back and forth.

fumigation The use of smoke or fumes to get rid of pests.

liability An obligation, responsibility, or debt.

mentor A wise or trusted counselor or teacher.

mulch A protective covering, usually of leaves, straw, or peat, placed around plants to prevent the evaporation of moisture, the freezing of roots, and the growth of weeds.

parquet A patterned wood surface (often used for floors).

portfolio A portable case for holding material, such as photographs or drawings, as well as the representative work a person keeps in it.

radon A colorless, radioactive, inert gaseous element formed by the decay of radium.

refrigerant A substance—such as air, ammonia, water, or carbon dioxide—that acts as a refrigerator's cooling agent.

scaffolding A temporary platform, supported from below or suspended from above, on which workers sit or stand when performing tasks high above the ground.

scale The proportion that an illustration or reproduction, especially a map or model, bears to the object that it represents.

seepage The process of water seeping or oozing.

soldering A means of joining or cementing two metallic parts together with melted tin or lead.

stucco A fine plaster used to decorate walls.

unethical Dishonorable, immoral.

voltmeter An instrument used to measure, in volts, the differences of potential between different points of an electrical circuit.

wattmeter An instrument used to measure electric power in watts.

INDEX

About the Author

Alice Beco grew up in eastern Canada and completed a degree in hotel and restaurant management at the University of Guelph, Ontario. While working for several hotels and then running her own B&B, Beco took some writing courses and began publishing newspaper and magazine articles in Canada, the United States, and the United Kingdom.

Photo Credits

Cover © www.istockphoto.com/Lynn Lynum; pp. 10, 13 © Bohemian Nomad Picturemakers/Corbis; p. 11 Longview/Taxi/Getty Images; p. 16 Billy Hustace/Photographer's Choice/Getty Images; pp. 20, 27 Photodisc Green/Getty Images; p. 21 © Virgo/Zefa/Corbis; p. 22 Didier Robcis/Stone/Getty Images; p. 25 Steve Winter/National Geographic/Getty Images; pp. 31, 35 © Philip Gould/Corbis; pp. 32, 43, 47, 78, 83, 88, 94, 98, 103 © AP/Wide World Photos; p. 37 © Bob Krist/Corbis; p. 44 Britt Erlanson/The Image Bank/Getty Images; p. 48 Courtesy of Katherine and David Boyd; p. 51 © Najlah Feanny/Corbis; pp. 56, 59 © H. Winkler/A.B./Corbis; p. 57 © Massimo Listri/Corbis; p. 61 Cindy Reiman; pp. 68, 70 Courtesy of ASHI; p. 73 © Ed Brock/Corbis; p. 80 © Kwame Zikomo/Superstock; pp. 84, 112 © Punchstock; p. 90 © Omni Photo Communications Inc./Index Stock Imagery; p. 92 Wayne Eastep/Photographer's Choice/Getty Images; p. 101 Christopher Bissell/Stone/Getty Images; pp. 108, 111 © Royalty-Free/Corbis; pp. 118, 121, 124 © Neat Productions; pp. 129, 130, 132 Courtesy of StagedHomes.com.

Designer: Evelyn Horovicz